Lynne Johnson's

Horse Lovers Vacation Guide

WESTERN, ENGLISH & TAKE YOUR OWN HORSE VACATIONS

– Rock Creek Pack Station, California

The purpose of this publication is to provide reference and source to a variety of different types of horseback vacations in one place. Lynne Johnson, publisher of the Horse Lovers Vacation Guide rides with many destinations each year to find new listings for the Guide. She cannot get to every place listed. We hope that you will have a great vacation, but we cannot be responsible for the quality of the program, horses, riding program, trails, accommodations, or other activities of your final selection. Please write or call to tell us about your trip. A form for doing this is found on page 151.

Horse Lovers Vacation Guide ISBN# 0-9656333-1-4 Library of Congress Catalog #98-092325

Cover photo: All 'round Ranch in Vernal, Utah provides adventure based educational programs on quality Quarter horses. The emphasis is on active learning while you trail ride or work cattle. See pages 76 and 120.
 – *Photo Debra Lex by permission of Wann Brown, All 'round Ranch.*

Photo Page 1: Rock Creek Pack Station crosses California's Pacific Crest Trail in the High Sierra. See pages 1 & 85.
 – *Photo Bill Hulit by permission of Rock Creek Pack Station.*

Also Available from Riding Vacations, Inc
• Riding Vacations Adventure Brochure
Brochure outlines places we have most recently visited or tested.
These are places we really have enjoyed and know you would too!

•Dude Ranch Vacations   • Wilderness Pack Trips
• Cowboy Vacations
Each include pricing and reservations.

Riding Vacations, Inc. • P.O. Box 502 • Richfield, OH 44286 • (330) 659-6007

The Wit's End Guest Ranch and Resort, Luxury at the End of the Wilderness

Wit's End Guest Ranch & Resort

254 County Road 500 • Bayfield, CO 81122 • (970) 884-4113

Folks, when you're at your wit's end, come to our Wit's End! We're looking forward to meeting you and getting to know you–

Jim, Lynn and the whole gang.

The Wild West Refined...
Saddle Up California Style!

Welcome to **The Alisal Guest Ranch & Resort**, California's premier guest ranch, operating since 1946. A 10,000 acre working cattle ranch with 73 California-ranch designed studio cottages and spacious suites. Located outside the quaint Danish town of Solvang, approximately 2 hours from Los Angeles and 40 minutes from Santa Barbara.

★ Two 18-hole championship golf courses with private or group lessons by PGA and LPGA professionals

★ Adventure-based team building from special horseback riding events to the outdoor challenge course

★ Miles of scenic horseback riding trails with breakfast and lunch rides and rodeos. Also, some of Southern California's best bass fishing and watersports on the 100-acre Alisal Lake

★ Seven tennis courts with private and group lessons.

1054 Alisal Road • Solvang, CA 93463 • (800) 425-4725 or (805) 688-6411

SOUTHWESTERN COLORADO

Schmittel Packing & Outfitting

Pack Trips in the Weminuche, La Garita and
Sangre de Cristo Wilderness areas.

800-648-8768

Colorado outfitters
registration #334

ARIZONA

Arizona's Riding Ranch

Flying E Ranch

2801 W. Wickenburg Way
Wickenburg, AZ 85390
(520) 684-2690
www.duderanch.org

COLORADO

American Safari Ranch

Rocky Mountain
Horseback Vacations
in Central Colorado

Box 128 • Fairplay, CO 80440 • **(719) 836-2431**

Stirrup a Few Memories

Cellular phones?

Forget about 'em.

Deadlines?

Never heard of 'em.

Traffic Jams?

Minimal, and a great way to make new friends.

Ride '99 says, "Hey, saddle up with us and explore the world's trails."

The American Quarter Horse Association is welcoming all breeds of horses and riders of all disciplines to participate in one of the most expansive trail blazing programs ever.

Ride '99 features rides on sites that are usually inaccessible to the public; some tour private ranches, while others explore national forests, recreational areas and parks. And when we throw in a meal and some entertainment to help you ease into the evening, that's a day at the office we're sure you'll enjoy.

Best of all, portions of Ride '99 proceeds will continue to benefit various charities selected by AQHA Affiliates who will be hosting the rides.

This way, therapeutic riding centers, equine health research and other charities share in the fun.

Saddle up and explore the world's trails!

For a schedule of Ride '99 events, call toll-free: 1-888-414-RIDE

AQHA's *Ride 99*

Saddle Up and Explore the World's Trails!

Destinations By Classification

Types of vacations available to those who want to spend vacation time
on the back of a good horse enjoying nature and the company of other horse lovers.

Riding Vacation Categories

Travel Planning

Symbols used throughout the book:

 Western riding   English riding   Take your own horse   Member of the
Dude Ranchers' Association

Using This Book...
A note to readers from Lynne Johnson.

"But you don't understand, I own a horse and want to take him with me", the call came one evening. I do understand, I too have owned horses for my lifetime and do indeed enjoy taking them along. The truth of the matter is that most people don't haul their horses more than 500 miles and even more no further than 100 miles, due to time constraints. This really limits your vacation area. By allowing your horse to have a vacation while you are away gives you the entire country and world to explore. On someone else's horses.

Finding places to ride is not easy. Most state tourist bureaus tell you of wonderful places to go to fish, swim and golf, without one word about horses. Horse magazines have a few listings in their ads here and there, but what you will find in this book are a variety of types of vacations both English and western, and for those of you who must haul your own horse along there are many destinations that allow you to take your horse. Look for the symbols to easily see at a glance what type of riding they offer.

— Lynne Johnson

As you tour through the book look for these symbols that show the type of riding facitities each destination offers.

🐴 Western riding 🐴 English riding 🐎 Take your own horse 🤠 Member of the Dude Ranchers' Association

Destinations By Location

For travel to a specific state or location.

United States

FOREIGN COUNTRIES

Planning Your Vacation

By Lynne Johnson

Your vacation starts long before you actually leave home. The planning of that trip is a big part, and can be fun. Look over the various categories in the book for the type of riding trip you are looking for.

Where do you wish to go? No two places are alike. Some may have similar programs but don't think that all dude ranches or all pack trips or all cattle drives are the same. You need to start out by making a list of what attributes you really want your destination to have. In many cases these need to be very general in nature. For instance, it is almost impossible to come up with the perimeters of wanting a horseback vacation in a specific city. They are not that plentiful to be everywhere. That is one of their charms. Instead pick a section of the country to start, the east or west.

When do you want to go? Is this an appropriate time to visit this area? Don't plan to pack into the highest mountains in April, there is too much snow in the passes.

What kind of a riding vacation do you want? In putting together this book we have tried to illustrate many different types of horseback trips. You can ride all day, learn a new riding skill, gain confidence in your riding skills, try out a different lifestyle, explore nature, learn about a new breed of horse, take your own horse....and more.

What do you want to do? Would you like some additional activities as well, list them. Many offer fishing, hiking, swimming.... If you have a non-rider companion there are many places that have all sorts of things for them to do as well.

What kind of lodging do you expect? Do you need special diets? They range from upscale fancy to back country tent camps. Ask for details about your lodging and meals before you go so you will not have any surprises.

How do I find out more about a place? Call, write or e-mail for brochures. As we travel this is one of the first things I study. Just to get the feel of the place. Even then it is not always just as you expected when you arrive. Perhaps the photos were too general and your brain reads more into what they show than is really there when you arrive. But this is a starting point.

Contact the destination and ask questions. Find out if there are references from past guests that you can contact. By doing so you can find things out from a guests perspective. Find out what delighted them about their vacation or what dismayed them. Don't call just one reference. Even the best place can have a guest that was unhappy. Usually they are people who didn't take the time to learn about what they were getting into ahead of time. A very rustic destination can be heaven for some and horror for others. In turn a fancy resort can be wonderful but for some too tame. If you would like input from the publisher of this book you can do so to get an unbiased opinion of our travels. Give us a call.

ANNUAL TRAIL RIDES

Annual rides bring specific ride dates for you to join a group, repeated each year as an annual event. Special activities are often set up, check with the individual ride organizer for details. Usually for privately owned horses but sometimes rentals are available.

MISSOURI
Golden Hills Trail Rides 🐂 🐎
and Resort
P.O. Box 98
Raymondville, MO 65555
(800)874-1157 or (417)457-6222

Season: April - October   Airport: Springfield, MO
Guest capacity: 1,200   Private groups available

1999 Rides:
April 18-24	May 2-8
May 16-22.	June 6-12
June 20-26,	July 11-17
Aug. 15-21,	Sept.5-11
Sept. 19-25,	Oct. 3-9
Oct. 17-23	Oct. 31-Nov. 6

Golden Hills Ranch, 5,100 acres of picturesque ranch land, crystal clear streams, forests, massive bluffs, caves, valleys, and wide open ranges, offers riding at all levels. Breathtaking scenery and spectacular wildlife make this trail ride and ranch memorable. Covered horse stalls, rental horses, lodging, campgrounds, water & electric, 3 hot meals daily, restroom & shower facilities, rodeo arena, recreation & exercise rooms, hayrides, barn dancing, cattle driving, calf penning & more.

MISSOURI
Wilderness Trailride 🐂 🐎
P.O. Box 90
Lesterville, MO 63654
(314) 637-2295   (314) 637-2504 fax
Season: April - November   Guest capacity: 200

Over 100 Miles of Trail in the Ozark Mountain Foothills
Cozy cottages with fireplaces or campground on the crystal clear Black River. Come for a scheduled wilderness trail ride, 2 - 7 days, or just come at your leisure and stay at the Lodge. Trails through scenic forests and streams. Rent stalls for your horses. Horses available for rental. Family style dining featuring delicious country cooking. Float the river, tennis, pool, hayrides and miniature golf.

NATIONWIDE
American Quarter Horse Association 🐎
P.O. Box 200
Amarillo, TX 79168
1-888-414-RIDE
e-mail: eroy@aqha.org   pshafer@aqha.org
Web: www.aqha.com
Season: April 1 to November 1 Guest capacity: unlimited

Organized Rides Scheduled Across the U.S. Spring Through Fall.
Provide your own horse unless the specific ride offers rental horses. Mostly western riding and trail riding. Rides may be guided or unguided. No stallions. Rates vary, but average around $30 to $40 per participant for the ride, meal and entertainment. Some rides offer wagons for non-riders.

16

OHIO
Palmerosa Horse Camp 🐎
19217 Keifel Road
Laurelville, OH 43135
(740) 385-3799   Jane Palmer
Season: Year-round

Guided trail rides to Box Canyons, Caves, Waterfalls and beautiful Rock Formations. Electric and non-electric well shaded campsites, showers, and fun shows. One price covers camping and food. Partial stays can be pro-rated if given advance notice. Custom rides can be arranged at anytime for 10 or more riders. Or join us anytime to ride on your own, for a week or a weekend.

OHIO
Smoke Rise Ranch Resort 🐎
Co. Road 92, P.O. Box 253
Murray City, OH 43144
(800)292-1732   (614)592-4077

Season: Year-round
Guest Capacity: 40 hookups; 175 primitive,
                6 cabins sleep 6 each

Ride on Your Own or Guided Trail Rides...
on 2,000 private acres with 100 miles of wooded trails linking the North Buckeye Trail, and 30,000 acres of National Forest. Stay in one of our cabins or camp. You'll find water and electric hookups along with modern restrooms and showers for your comfort. We offer a cattle ranch, trails, indoor and outdoor arenas, team pennings, roping, barrels, horse rentals, clinics, Meals at our dining lodge, swimming pool, hot tub, fishing and a child's playground.

OKLAHOMA
Indian Mounds Camp 🐎
HC 60, Box 62
Clayton, OK 74536
(918) 569-4761
e-mail trailleader@juno.com
Web: www.indianmoundshorsecamp.com
Season: Year-round

Palmerosa '99 Ride Schedule	
May 1	– Horse & Tack Auction
June 4-6	– OHC State Ride
June 20-26	– Organized Ride
July 9-11	– Ladies Weekend
July 23-25	– 6th Annual Mule Ride
Aug. 7-9	– Father & Sons Ride
Aug. 20-23	– Singles Weekend
Sept.12-18	– Organized Ride
October 1-3 –	
	Mule, Horse & Tack Auction,
	7th Annual Fall Mule Ride
Oct. 8-11	– Organized Ride

1999 Annual Trail Rides & Clinics	
April 9-11	– Bring in the Sp[ring
May 1-4	– Ray Hunt Clinic
May 8-9	– Roy Cooper Roping Clinic
May 28-31	– Memorial Day Ride
June 7-12	– Natural Horsemanship Clinic
June 25-27	– Summer Sizzler
July 2-5	– July 4th Celebration Ride
July 25-30	– 6 Days in the Saddle
July 28	– Moonlight Ride
Aug. 14	– Bluegrass Festival
Aug. 21-22	– Overnight Ride
Sept. 3-6	– Labor Day Weekend Ride
Sept.18-19	– Overnight Ride
Oct. 8-10	– Fall Color Ride
Nov. 6	– Auction & Awards Banquet

1999 Annual Trail Rides	
March 12-13-14	– Early Bird Ride
April 16-17-18	– April "Showers" Ride
May 21-22-23-24	– Memorial Day Ride
June 18-19-20	– Summer Fun
July 1-2-3-4	– Fourth of July Ride
September 3-4-5-6	– Labor Day Ride
October 15-16-17	– 17th Fall Color
October 22-23-24	– Fall Encore

Indian Mounds Camp is Built on the Site of an Ancient Indian Village.
Located in the scenic Kiamichi Mountains of southeastern Oklahoma there are over 100 miles of well-marked trail to ride from your shady campsite. Room for the largest horse trailer, with full hookups, showers, a 40'X120' pavilion, all-weather roads and close to area restaurants and groceries. Come at your leisure or join one of the annual rides – Spring Dogwood-Ride-April 11-12; Fall Color Ride-October 15-17. We do it all – guided rides, hot home-cooked meals. Clubs and groups welcome.

BED & BREAKFAST

Bed and Breakfast establishments reflect the care and interests of their owner / operators. Some are historic buildings, renovated to reflect the time of their construction. All evoke a feeling of warmth and hospitality. They have become the place of choice for many when seeking overnight lodging and gone on to become major destinations for others.

CALIFORNIA
The Homestead
41110 Road 600
Ahwahnee, CA 93601
(209) 683-0495

Season: February 1 - January 8

Romantic, Private Cottages AND You Can Bring Your Own Horse!
Our adobe, stone and cedar cottages are nestled in a forest of mature oaks, overlooking a panoramic Sierra view. Horses are stabled in 10' X 12' partially covered pipe corral stalls. Accommodations offer a living room with fireplace and TV, fully equipped kitchen, separate bedroom and bathrooms. The owners will help you plan your riding in nearby Yosemite and Sierra National Forests.

IDAHO
The Kingston 5 Ranch Bed & Breakfast
P.O. Box 130
42297 Silver Valley Road
Kingston, ID 83839
(800)254-1852 or (208)682-4862
(208)682-9445 fax
e-mail: k5ranch@nidlink.com/
Web: www.nidlink.com/~k5ranch

Season: Year-round
Guest capacity: 4
Airport: Spokane, WA

B&B With a Touch of Country Elegance...A Perfect Stop On Your Glacier Loop Tour.
1 mile south of I-90. Rates; $85 per night for two riders includes stabling your horses and a *Wonderful* Large Country Breakfast. Upgrades to suites with in-room fireplaces, bath and jacuzzi plus our outdoor spa. Indoor/outdoor stalls, individual pastures, round pen, 200'X100' arena and the famous 1,000 mile Silver County Trail System. Activities nearby: rental horses, whitewater rafting, mountain biking on "Trail of the Hiawatha". Winter downhill & x-country skiing and snowmobiling.

IDAHO
Moose Creek Ranch ⬆
P.O. Box 350
Victor, ID 83455
(800)676-0075 or (208)787-2784
Web: www.webfactor.com/mooscrk/

Season: June 1- September 30
Guest capacity: 35
Airport: Idaho Falls, ID

Breathtaking Rides Await You in the Heart of the Majestic Teton Mountains.
Seasoned wranglers provide personal guidance to experienced and beginning riders. Little tykes have their own programs and day care. Other activities include square dancing, an evening at a western show and a raft trip on the Snake River. Variety of accommodations/all ages welcome. Homecooked family style meals served in the main lodge or outdoors. Indoor heated pool, sauna and hot tub round out our comfortable relaxed mountain home. Yellowstone 1-1/2 hours drive and the night life and shopping of Jackson Hole, Wyoming only 30 minutes away.

INDIANA
Coneygar 🐴
54835 County Rd 33
Middlebury, IN 46540
(219) 825-5707

Season: Year-round   Guest capacity: 8

Enjoy Our 40 Acre Horse Farm in the Hilly, Wooded Middlebury Countryside.
Bed & breakfast and overnight stabling on our horse farm near I-80/90 in northern Indiana Amish country. Enjoy antiques, fireplaces and a full breakfast. Near gift shops, restaurants, horse and carriage auctions, golf, museums, and the Shipshewana Flea Market.

MICHIGAN
Cedar Lodge & Stables ⬆🐴
47000 52nd St.
P.O. Box 218
Lawrence, MI 49064-0218
(616)674-8071
e-mail: info@cedarlodge.com
Web: www.cedarlodge.com

Season: Year-round
Guest capacity: 2-50
Airport: Kalamazoo, MI

Cedar Lodge and Cedar Lodge Hunter/Jumper Stables.
Located in the fruit belt of lower Michigan on 160 acres of rolling recreational lands with a private 12 acre fishing lake, special guest rooms await those who are looking for a relaxing visit to a hunter stable. Miles of trails, cross country course, jumping ring, indoor arena, private lessons, instructor certification, boarding. Loads of good fishing and hiking. Only 3 miles off I-94. Also full service children's riding summer camp. Write or call for brochure.

NEVADA
The Stonehouse Country Inn 🐎
Hwy 290
P.O. Box 77
Paradise Valley, NV 89426
(702)578-3530
Web: home.sprynet.com/sprynet/stonehouse.

Season: Year-round   Guest capacity: 18   Airport: Reno or Elko, NV

Truly A Trip To Paradise!
We have six spacious guest rooms with views from every room and large paddocks with shelter and safe fencing. Ride through the Santa Rosa Mountains and finish your day with a sumptuous meal surrounded by green lawns and blooming gardens. Reservations only, please.

NORTH CAROLINA
Burnside Plantation 🐎
960 Burnside Road
Henderson, NC 27536
(252)438-7688
(252)430-7097 fax

e-mail: burnside@gloryroad.net
Web: burnside.host4u.com

Season: Year-round   Guest capacity: 4   Airport: Raleigh-Durham, NC

Trail Riding.
Visit our fully restored 19th Century Guest House on an 18th Century plantation. Two bedroom, private baths, kitchen facilities, central air, large stone fireplace, stocked fishing pond. Four stalls are available in a restored 18th century barn, surrounded by board fenced pastures. Miles of trails. Premium fishing and sailing on nearby Kerr Lake. Horse owners responsible for their own horse care and feed. Neg. Coggins test, signed waiver of liability and deposit required.

OHIO
Heartland Country Resort 🍽 🥾 🐎
2994 Township Road 190
Fredericktown, OH 43019
(800)230-7030
(419)768-9300
Web: www.bbhost.com/heartland

Season: Year-round   Guest capacity: 40   Airport: Columbus, OH

**Heartland Country Resort is Rated "Excellent"
by the American Bed & Breakfast Association.**
And a riding stable with many registered horses offering walk-trot-canter riding. Recreation and relaxation abound, with riding in arenas or on our own wooded trails, swim in the heated pool, play pool in the recreation room or cross-country ski over the rolling countryside, compete in a game of basketball, ping pong, or horseshoes, lounge on the deck or screened porch, have a candle lit meal in the 1878 dining room, watch movies in the sitting room, AND unwind in your private Jacuzzi at day's end. Near many state forest trail system trailheads.

SOUTH CAROLINA
Mt. Carmel Farm Bed & Breakfast 🐎
Rt. 2, Box 580 A
Walterboro, SC 29488
(803)538-5770
Season: Year round   Airport: Charleston, SC

Visit Our Relaxing, Laid Back, Put Your Feet Up B&B.
You'll feel at home the minute you enter our cozy old farm house. Your choice of rooms with 2 double beds or a queen sized bed, each with private bath. Our guests love our farm dinners and delicious breakfast. They are encouraged to take along a doggy bag for the trail. We provide overnight stabling for horses. Or enjoy ours for lessons and supervised riding, beginner to advanced. Enjoy our above ground pool or cozy fireplace. While you are here, visit the nearby SC Artisan Center, or Middletown Gardens in Charleston. One of our guests described their stay as a visit "Back to Granmas".

SOUTH DAKOTA
Bunkhouse Bed & Breakfast 🐎
14630 Lower Spring Creek Road
Hermosa, SD 57744
(888)756-5462
(605)342-5462

Season: May 1-December 31
Airport: Rapid City, SD   Capacity: 10

Working Ranch Bed & Breakfast With Stabling and Limited Camping.
Load up your favorite horse and hang your hat at our working ranch B&B. Ride in the land where buffalo, deer, antelope, and elk roam free (where cowboys and Indians still make their living off the land.) Follow well marked trails, or set off on your own in Custer State Park, Badlands National Park, or on our ranch. Drift off to peaceful sleep listening to the creek and coyotes, awaken to the smell of fresh coffee and be welcomed to our sumptuous "all you can eat" breakfast. Trail maps and guided rides available. Couples, singles, families or small groups welcome.

TENNESSEE
Sweet Annie's Bed, Breakfast & Barn 🐎
7201 Cumberland Drive
Fairview, TN 37062
(615)799-8833 phone/fax
Web: www.bbonlin.com/tn/sweetannies/index.html

Season: Year-round   Guest capacity: 4   Airport: Nashville, pickup available

Relax and Get Away From It All Or Get Into the Heart of Music City!
A contemporary home with lots of windows. The guest rooms are light, airy and comfy. Full country breakfast. Bring your horses, we have stalls, paddocks and pasture. Ride or hike in Bowie Nature Park (800 acres of marked trail), Natchex Trace Parkway trails, and Montgomery Bell State Park. Swimming pool in season, hot tub, and nearby - Nashville, the Loveless Cafe, Hermitage (Andrew Jackson's home), Golf courses, and Shelbyville (Tennessee Walking Horse Celebration).

TEXAS
Knolle Farm & Ranch 🐴🐴📷
Barn, Bed & Breakfast

Rt. 1, Box 81, Farm Road 70
Sandia, TX 78383
(512)547-2546   (512)547-3934 fax
Web: www.knolle.com

Season: Year-round   Guest capacity: 18   Airport: Corpus Christi, TX

Bed, Barn and Breakfast in a Renovated Historic 1939 Dairy Barn.

Knolle Jersey Farms boasted the "World's Largest Jersey Herd" for over 60 years, now it pampers guests. Nestled in the Nueces River Valley amidst towering oaks and lush, rolling fields. Western & English riding, cattle roundups. Guests with private horses find spacious barns, paddocks, 2 riding arenas, and acres of trails. Upscale guest cottages are filled with antiques, & full kitchens. Fishing, canoeing, sailing, game room, golf carts, and guided hunting on premises. Catered gourmet meals. Birdwatching, located on the Great Texas Coastal Birding Trail. Fun for all wanting individual attention.

WASHINGTON
Silver Ridge Ranch 📷

P.O. Box 644
Easton, WA 98925
(509)656-0275   (509)656-2442 fax

Season: April to October   Guest capacity: campground - 61 spaces, lodge - 22
Airport: Seattle / Tacoma

Silver Ridge Ranch Offers a Bed and Breakfast and Campgrounds.

Silver Ridge Ranch is located one hour east of Seattle in the beautiful Cascade Mountains. We have private corrals for your horses, RV / tent sites and our beautiful lodge. Ride from the ranch on mountain trails to lakes, and streams with breathtaking views. Easy access to the John Wayne Trail. When the snow flies come rent a snowmobile as a guest of our lodge. Contact us for information on group retreats, weddings, family reunions, business meetings or picnics.

WEST VIRGINIA
Swift Level 🐴🐴📷

Rt 2, Box 269
Lewisburg, WV 24901
(540) 645-1155

Season: April to November   Guest capacity: 12   Airport: Greenbrier Valley Airport

Ride the Appalachians.

Enjoy riding through the heartland of one of America's best kept secrets, in the Appalachian Mountains of West Virginia, on our world famous horses and Connemara ponies. Experience breathtaking views from high elevations. Pure mountain streams flanked by natural Rhododendron and lush farms in fertile valleys with pastures filled with cattle and sheep. Make this your opportunity to visit our part of the world. A place where Appalachian hospitality and culture await you.

Symbols used throughout the book:

🐴 Western riding provided   🐴 English riding provided   📷 Private horses welcome

CAMPS - Youth

NATIONWIDE
American Camping Association
5000 State Road 67 North
Martinsville, IN 46151   (800)428-2267 or (765) 342-8456
e-mail:msnider@aca-camps.org   Web: www.aca~camps.org

Guide to ACA-Accredited Camps
To purchase a complete listing of all 2,000 accredited camps – call 800-428-2267 or our website.

CALIFORNIA
Monte Vista Horsemanship Camp 🐎🐴
2 School Way
Watsonville, CA 95076
(408)724-9382   (408)722-6003 fax
Season: June 15 - August 15 Guest capacity: 50 Ages: 10-17 Airport: San Jose, CA, pickup available

Make Your Dreams Come True.
Monte Vista Horsemanship Camp has a riding program to fit your level, English and Western. Each exciting and fun filled week will be packed with "horsey" activities, including trail rides, arena instruction, vaulting, jumping, horse science, gymkana, roping, goat tying, and working cattle.

MICHIGAN
Cedar Lodge 🐎🐴
P.O. Box 218, - 47000 52nd St.
Lawrence, MI 49064-0218
(616) 674-8071
e-mail: info@cedarlodge.com   Web: www.cedarlodge.com
Season: Year-round   Guest capacity: 2-50   Ages: 7-17   Airport: Kalamazoo, MI

Riding Summer Camp for Boys and Girls 7-17.
All riding disciplines with hunt seat and stadium jumping our specialty. Western riding, trail riding, horseback overnights, vaulting, grooming, horse care, and instructor certification. Full program summer camp with swimming, arts/crafts, music, archery, biking and many other programs available. Write or call for brochure.

NORTH CAROLINA
Camp Winding Gap 🐎
Rt 1, Box 56
Lake Toxaway, NC 28747
(828) 966-4520 or (888)CWG-CAMP   (828) 883-8720 fax
e-mail: campwgap@sitcom.net   Web: www.campwindinggap.com
Season: June - August   Guest capacity: 75   Ages: 6-17   Airport: Asheville, NC

Camp Winding Gap is a Private Summer Camp for Boys and Girls.
Offering a variety of activities including an exceptional English and Western riding program. Trail riding as ability permits, lunch and supper rides, overnights and 2 or 3-day Pack & Trail Trips. Riding is included in the tuition and staffed by highly trained and certified instructors. Safety is stressed with use of proper clothing and helmets. Certification and patches awarded for all levels of riding from elementary to overnight rider. A rodeo is held during the middle 3-week session each summer.

CAMPGROUNDS

Take your horse on vacation. Campgrounds range from very primitive to luxurious. Many have electric and water hookups for your RV, box stalls for your horse and resort facilities with a variety of activities for the whole family. Some also offer private cabins or rental horses.

ILLINOIS
Bear Branch Horse Camp
P.O. Box 40, HWY 145
Eddyville, IL 62928
(616)672-4249   (618)672-4739 fax
e-mail: manders@shawnee.link.com

Season open: Year-round
Airport: Nashville, KY
Guest capacity: 4 cabins,
    80 campsites w/hookups,
    40 acres of primitive camping

**Bear Branch Horse Camp,
Outfitter, Log Cabin Restaurant
and the Ultimate Trail Ride.**

Overlooking Lusk Creek Canyon, one of the most scenic areas in the 275,000 acre Shawnee National Forest. Ride our lush forest trails, ford rocky creeks, travel down rock canyons, circle & climb high bluffs under waterfalls into large caves, you'll see why this is the home of the Ultimate Trail Ride. Featuring a Rustic Log Cabin Restaurant, tack shop, general store, a barn with 40 bedded horse stalls. Heated and air conditioned shower house with laundry facilities, dump station, a 2 acre pond for swimming and fishing, and cabins for rent as well as trail horses. Trail Guide in camp at all times.

ILLINOIS
Circle B Ranch
P.O. Box 144
Eddyville, IL 62928
(618)672-4748

Season: April 1 to November 30
Guest capacity: 19 campsites
Airports: Marion, IL and Paducah, KY

In the Heart of Shawnee National Forest's Most Scenic Trail Riding.
Huge rock formations, secluded canyons with towering bluffs, tumbling streams, hilly timbered trails and caves. Shady graveled campsites with water, electricity, and pipe pens at each site. Rec building with modern bathrooms, showers, lounge area, picnic tables, laundromat. Trail guides available. Bring your own horses. Restaurants nearby. Outstanding facilities.

KENTUCKY
Double "J" Stables and Campgrounds 🐴 🐎

P.O. Box 6, Lincoln School Road
Mammoth Cave, KY 42259
(502) 286-8167   (800)730-HRSE (in Kentucky)
Season: March to October   Location: Near Cave City, KY

70 Miles of Trail into the Mammoth Cave National Park, Start at Our Campground!
We are a licensed outfitter for the Mammoth Cave National Park with facilities for horse owners
to board their horses and camp. Our campgrounds have sites with both water and electric
hookup and rustic sites. We also have horse rentals featuring 1 hour, 2 hour and 1/2 day guided
rides. The park visitor center is only 15 minutes away with cave tours every day. Nearby Nolin
Lake is a great place to get away to with it's beaches, swimming, and picnic areas. Join us, the
trails are some of the most beautiful you will find anywhere.

KENTUCKY
Wrangler's Campground 🐎

100 Van Morgan Drive
Golden Pond, KY 42211
(800)LBL-7077   (502)924-2087 fax   Web: www.lbl.org
Season: Year-round   Airport: Nashville, TN

Wranglers Campground at Land Between the Lakes, National Recreation Area.
Ride along 75 miles of horse trails and wagon roads. Our campground features camping shelters,
electric sites, bath houses, stalls and stables, an outpost supply center, tack and farrier service.

MISSISSIPPI
Big Sand Campground, Inc. 🐎

c/o David E. Strong
3412 Reedtown Road
Utica, MS 39175
(601)885-8068   (601) 636-6369 fax
Season: Year-round   Guest capacity: 12 sites w/e - 14 sites water only - many tent sites

Ride the Historic Natchez Trace Parkway.
This is a private campground in a quiet, peaceful setting for fun or relaxing. Sites for equestrian and
non-equestrian guests. Clean restrooms and showers, dump station, large arena, two fenced pastures
and a six stall barn. Big Sand Creek borders the camp for wading, picnicking, photographing wildlife
and birdwatching. Direct access to the Natchez Trace National Scenic Trail for riding and hiking. Well
marked trails through pine and hardwood forest, rolling hills, deep ravines and creek crossings.

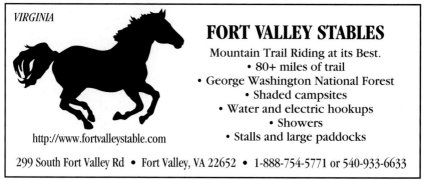

VIRGINIA

FORT VALLEY STABLES

Mountain Trail Riding at its Best.
- 80+ miles of trail
- George Washington National Forest
- Shaded campsites
- Water and electric hookups
- Showers
- Stalls and large paddocks

http://www.fortvalleystable.com

299 South Fort Valley Rd • Fort Valley, VA 22652 • 1-888-754-5771 or 540-933-6633

OHIO
Palmerosa Horse Camp

19217 Keifel Road
Laurelville, OH 43135
(614)385-3799

Season: Year-round

Camp Here or Rent a Bunkhouse or Cabin, and Ride Through the Scenic Hocking Hills.
Ride in caves and box canyons, see waterfalls and large rock formations. Our scenic tall hills, ravines and deep forests will convince you that southern Ohio is not just flat farmland! Write for literature on our annual organized rides (see "Annual Trail Rides" for dates). Electric and non-electric sites, well shaded campsites, showers and a lot of fun. Try our spacious new cabin or bunkhouses.

OHIO
Smoke Rise Ranch Resort

Co Road 92, P.O. Box 253
Murray City, OH 43144
(800)292-1732

Season: Year-round
Guest capacity: 40 hookups; 175 primitive; 6 cabins sleep 6 each

Western Style Fun For the Whole Family.
Ride on your own or enjoy guided trail rides, on 2,000 private acres with 100 miles of trails linking the North Buckeye Trail, and 30,000 acres of National Forest. Our campground has water and electric hook-ups along with modern restrooms and showers for your comfort. Cabins are available. We offer a cattle ranch, trails, indoor and outdoor arenas, team pennings, roping, clinics, barrels, horse rentals, meals at our dining lodge, swimming pool, hot tub, fishing & a child's playground.

OKLAHOMA
Indian Mounds Camp

HC 60, Box 62
Clayton, OK 74536
(918)569-4761
e-mail: trailleader@juno.com
Web: www.indianmoundshorsecamp.com

Season: Year-round

Indian Mounds Camp is Built on the Site of an Ancient Indian Village.
Located in the scenic Kiamichi Mountains of southeastern Oklahoma there are over

100 miles of well-marked trail to ride from your shady campsite. Room for the largest horse trailer, with full hookups, showers, a 40'X120' pavilion, all-weather roads and close to area restaurants and groceries. Come at your leisure or join the many annual rides – Spring Dogwood-Ride-May 1-3; Fall Color Ride-October 16-18. Guided rides, hot home-cooked meals. Clubs and groups welcome.

Tip: Horses unaccustomed to traveling often refuse to drink strange water.
Purchase 5 gallon tanks to take their water along with you.

PENNSYLVANIA

Artillery Ridge Campgrounds & the National Riding Stable ♞ 🐴

610 Taneytown Road
Gettysburg, PA 17325
(717)334-1288

Season: April 1-November 30   Airport: Harrisburg, PA

Ride the Historic Gettysburg Battlefield.
Feel a sense of history as you ride the battlefield as our forefathers did. Bring your own horses, we have box stalls and corrals to stable them. Or ride one of ours on a guided ride across the battle fields. Try our 2 hour ride accompanied by a Licensed Battlefield Guide that includes the Pickett's Charge area. We have 112 electric and water sites and acres of non-hookup sites. Your camping includes FREE hot showers, swimming pool, stocked fishing and much more.

PENNSYLVANIA

Flying W Ranch ♞ 🐴

Star Route 2
Box 150
Tionesta, PA 16353
(814)463-7663

Season: April to Mid-December
Guest capacity: 100
Airport: Pittsburgh, PA

A Dude Ranch for Horse People with Many Options.
Enjoy our scenic cabins and long rides through the Allegheny Mountains. Ride our

horses or bring your own, stabling available. Park your camper in our campgrounds or forest wilderness camps. Join our yearly Organized Trail Rides. Enjoy the Allegheny Mountain Championship Rodeo or American Indian Pow-Wow. Schedule a mountain pack trip. Send your child to our Summer Camp. Plan an Adult Getaway Weekend. Something for all riders.

SOUTH DAKOTA

Mountain Meadow Resort ♞ 🐴

11321 Gillette Prairie Road
Hill City, SD 57745-6526
(605)574-2636   (605)574-4891 fax

Season: May 15-September 30
Guest capacity: 4 cabins, (5 people each); 25 campsites, (25 families)
Airport: Rapid City, SD

The Horseman's Resort!
Explore the Black Hills from the Mountain Meadow Resort located at Deerfield Lake. You will find excellent facilities for yourself and your horses. Stay in the housekeeping cabins or campground which has electrical sites and full hookups, fire pits, water and a bathhouse. Various size corrals house horses. The trail system is well mapped, no guiding necessary. Trails from 4-15 miles long with points of interest along each trail. Close to Mt. Rushmore, Crazy Horse and Custer State Park.

TENNESSEE
Wild Heart Ranch
1070 Old Sewanee Road (actual address)
P.O. Box 130 (mailing address)
Sewanee, TN 37375
(423)837-0849
Season: Year round   Location: One hour from Chattanooga   Guest capacity: 48-100

Our Campground is Private, Quiet and Secluded. The Silence is Deafening!
Bordering 7,000 acres of the Franklin State Forest you'll find a wide variety of trails from easy top riding to steep terrain. Enjoy spectacular mountain views, waterfalls, lakes, creeks and caves. Our campsites offer electric and water, a bathhouse and pavilion. Large trailers are easily accommodated. Or attractive lakeside cabins and a mountainside lodge are available. Stable in our new horse barn. The country store on site has whatever you need. Come ride, fish the stocked lakes, hike, and enjoy.

VIRGINIA
Fort Valley Stable
299 S. Fort Valley Road
Fort Valley, VA 22652
(888)-754-5771   (540)933-6633   (540)933-6634 fax
e-mail: fvs@fortvalleystable.com   Web: www.fortvalleystable.com/
Season: Year-round   Guest capacity: 25 rigs-main camp, 50 overflow

Bring Your Horse or Rent One of Ours.
Mountain trail riding at it's best on over 80 miles of riding trails. We are surrounded by the George Washington National Forest, outstanding scenic panoramas. Trails access right off our property. Shaded camp sites, water & electric hook-ups, showers. We can accommodate large horse trailers or sites for tent camping. Picket line or your portable corral, or rent our stalls or large paddocks.

WASHINGTON
Silver Ridge Ranch
P.O. Box 644
Easton, WA 98925
(509)656-0275   (509)656-2442 fax
Season: April to October
Guest capacity: campground - 61 spaces, lodge - 22
Airport: Seattle / Tacoma

Silver Ridge Ranch Offers a Bed and Breakfast and Campgrounds.
Silver Ridge Ranch is located one hour east of Seattle in the beautiful Cascade Mountains. We have private corrals for your horses, RV / tent sites and our beautiful lodge. Ride from the ranch on mountain trails to lakes, and streams with breathtaking views. Easy access to the John Wayne Trail. When the snow flies come rent a snowmobile as a guest of our lodge. Contact us for information on group retreats, weddings, family reunions, business meetings or picnics.

CATTLE DRIVES & ROUNDUPS

Work with real cowboys to move the herd to new pasture. Try out the lifestyle on the range.

ARIZONA

The Horseshoe Ranch on Bloody Basin Road

HCR 34, Box 5005
Mayer, AZ 86333
(520) 632-8813
e-mail: hranch@primenet.com
Web: www.primenet.com/~hranch/
Season: September - June
Airport: Phoenix, AZ   Guest capacity: 12

Ranch for Experienced Riders, Become Part of the Team That Rides For the Horseshoe Brand.

Experienced riders come to do what they have never done before – work cattle from the saddle of a cattle-savvy ranch horse. Riders find doing real cowboy work the "Ultimate High". 70,000 acres of mesas, canyons and mountains in snow-free Arizona. Saddle up and do what needs done for the day, sorting, searching for strays, gathering driving, roping, riding fence, branding and doctoring. Then shower off the trail dust in your own private ranch house room and enjoy a hearty ranch meal.

COLORADO

Buffalo Horn Ranch

13825 County Rd. 7
Meeker, CO 81641
(970) 878-5450   (970) 878-4088 fax
Web: www.buffalohorn.com
Season: May - August
Guest capacity: 30
Airport: Grand Junction, CO

Help Herd Cattle on Our 20,000+ Acre Working Cattle Ranch

in spectacular northwest Colorado. Novices to old hands will have fun helping our cowboys move and doctor the cattle as they change pastures. You'll enjoy lunch on the trail or return to our spacious new lodge for gourmet buffet meals, Western style. Relax in the evening in the spa or around a bonfire, enjoy a game of pool, big screen TV and other amenities of the lodge. Make reservations now for great scenery, friendly folks, fine food, and outdoor fun at its finest! Call or write for additional information.

COLORADO
Lost Valley Ranch 🤠

29555 Goose Creek Road, Box HL
Sedalia, CO 80135
(303) 647-2311
e-mail:lostranch@alol.com
Web: www.ranchweb.com/lost

Season: March 1-December 1
Guest capacity: 90
Airport: Colorado Springs, CO

Discover Our Year 'round Authentic Working Cattle/Horse Ranch.
Just 80 miles from Denver or Colorado Springs. Blaze new trails while exploring 40,000 acres of the Rocky Mountains. Year 'round riding, cattle roundups, special horsemanship weeks, weekly rodeos and Orvis fishing schools. AAA rated "4 Diamonds". Cabin-suites with fireplace. Weekly all-inclusive adult rates: $1,695 (summer); $700-$1,290 (fall and spring).

COLORADO
Roubideau Western Adventures 🤠

3680 Cedar Rd.
Delta, CO 81416
(888)878-9378
Season: Branding - April through May
            Cattle Drives and Chuckwagon trips
            Cowcamps - June - October
Airport: Grand Junction, or Montrose, CO

RIDE THE RANGE and Share the Joys of life at Summer Cow Camp.
Ride with the cowboys and cowgirls as you roundup and trail cattle, pack salt, and check fence, while enjoying the fresh air, wildlife, and beautiful scenery of western Colorado. Each day is a new adventure. Our ranches offer over 150,000 acres of pristine views, with altitudes from 5,700 to 10,000 ft. Move 2,500 head through areas of grass, sage, pines, aspen and mountain trails.

COLORADO
Wilderness Trails Ranch 🤠

1766 County Road 302
Durango, CO 81301
(800)527-2624   (970)247-0722
e-mail and Web: www.wildernesstrails.com
Season: September 28 - October 7 1998
Guest capacity: 18   Airport: Durango, CO

Join Our Fall Cattle Roundup, September 27 - October 3.
Join us for an authentic cattle roundup. We only take 18 experienced adult riders and may spend 6 hours a day in the saddle. The terrain can be challenging but the scenery spectacular. We return to the ranch in the evenings for specially prepared dinners and a good nights rest in our comfortable, log cabins with private baths and comfortable beds.

COLORADO
Wit's End Ranch 🐎
254 County Road 500
Bayfield, CO 81122
(970) 884-4113
Season: Year-round   Guest capacity: 66   Airport: Durango, CO

Weekly Cattle Drives
One or more days a week we go to our lower elevation cow operation. You can push the cattle, get in on our spring and fall round up, branding, or move our cattle across the 6,000 acre ranch. Spend the day or overnight. Chuckwagon grub included. Cattle drive and horse drive included when you are a guest at the ranch. Please see color photos of our ranch on pages 4 and 5.

MONTANA/WYOMING
Schively Ranch 🐎
1062 Rd 15, Box HL
Lovell, WY 82431   Reservations 800-648-8768
Season: April - May and October - November   Airport: Billings, MT   Guest capacity: 17

Be a Cowboy! Join Our Genuine Cattle Drive Adventures!
Ride the range on a real cattle drive, ride over thousands of acres of rolling foothills. In the Spring trail cattle from our Wyoming ranch to high summer pastures in Montana where the grazing is lush. In fall round 'em up and drive 'em back to Wyoming. Drives start and end on Saturday.

WYOMING

THE WEST
The Way You Want It!
Spend a week with
America's last hero.

Terry Bison Ranch Resort
BISON DRIVE
Explore historic Blackfeet & Crow sites.
Stay in our authentic bunkhouse.
Trophy trout fishing in our private lake
and don't forget our genuine Chuckwagon Dinners.
Space is limited – call 1-800-319-4171 for details.

CHRISTIAN DESTINATIONS

Enjoy the beauty of God's natural kingdom while in a Christian atmosphere. Many places offer Bible studies and special programs for your group, directed at families, youth, marriage encounter, and church or family retreats. Enjoy the glory of God's kingdom. Singles, families and couples.

COLORADO
Wind River Ranch

P.O. Box 3410
Estes Park, CO 80517
(970)586-4212 (970)586-2255 fax
e-mail: wolff@windriverranch.com
Web: www.windriverranch.com

Season: June to September   Guest capacity: 50   Airport: Denver, CO

A Vacation With a Purpose.
Wind River is a Christian family guest ranch. Trail rides into the Rocky Mountain National Park as well as Roosevelt National Forest. Located in the magnificent Tahosa Valley at 9,200 feet with spectacular views of Long's Peak. Variety of rides to accommodate the skills of each rider. Wrangler breakfast, steak cook out, and hayrides for the entire family. Kids program also available.

VIRGINIA
Shenandoah Springs
Country Inn & Retreats

P.O. Box 770
Madison, VA 22727
(540)923-4300

Season: Year-round   Guest capacity: 120   Airport: Charlottesville or Dulles

Come Enjoy Our Farm and Historic Pre-Civil War Farmhouse With Us!
Relax and enjoy 1,000 acres of forest, meadows, bridle trails and scenic views. A Christian retreat center for groups, or bed & breakfast for couples or families and child's summer camp. Lodging in our Historic Farmhouse and newer cabins. Conference rooms for 30 to 150 people. Casual, shaded bridle trails with mountain, lake and wilderness beauty. Fishing, & canoeing, hiking, basketball, volleyball, biking, swimming, tubing, archery, and riflery. In winter cross-country skiing, sledding and ice skating.

CORPORATE OR FAMILY RETREATS

Get away to a quiet place with room for the whole group to concentrate on catching up with business or for a family to catch up on how the years have passed and the family has grown. Activities for all. Corporate meeting rooms and staff available.

ARKANSAS
Scott Valley Resort and Guest Ranch 🐎🤠

Box 1447-HL
Mountain Home, AR 72653
(501)425-5136
Web: www.scottvalley.com
Season: March-November   Guest capacity: 65   Airport: Springfield, MO or Little Rock, AR

Missouri Foxtrotters For Your Riding Pleasure!
Whether you are an experienced rider or novice, the Coopers have placed quality horseback riding as a priority on their ranch. These are "home-grown" superb horses, YOU actually get to ride! Rides are commensurate to ability, and we have one just right for you! Nestled in the Ozark Mountains, you get all the beautiful scenery without the concern of altitude sickness. Spring and fall are geared for the serious rider, (some all adult weeks) summer is aimed at family fun, lots of it!

COLORADO
Buffalo Horn Ranch 🐎🐴

13825 County Rd. 7
Meeker, CO 81641
(970)878-5450   (970)878-4088 fax
Web: www.buffalohorn.com

Season: May - December   Guest capacity: 30 - 50   Airport: Grand Junction, CO

Reserve Our Entire Facility for Your Function...
and take advantage of our spacious new lodge with all the amenities to support your family group or a focused meeting! Explore our 20,000+ acre working horse/cattle ranch on horseback, on foot, or in a 4-wheel drive. Enjoy panoramic views. Sign up with certified instructors and improve your shooting, fishing, or riding skills while you're here. Engage in special activities like a cattle drive. Let us customize your event to make it truly memorable! Please call or write for additional information.

COLORADO
Lost Valley Ranch 🐎🤠

29555 Goose Creek Road, Box HL
Sedalia, CO 80135
(303)647-2311   (303)647-2315 fax
e-mail: lostranch@aol.com
Web: www.ranchweb.com/lost

Season: March 1-December 1   Guest capacity: 95 Airport: Denver or Colorado Springs, CO

Discover Our Year-'round Authentic Working Cattle/Horse Ranch.
Just 80 miles from Denver or Colorado Springs. Blaze new trails while exploring 26,000 acres of the Rocky Mountains. We have year 'round riding, cattle roundups, special horsemanship weeks, weekly rodeos and an Orvis fly-fishing school. AAA rated "4 Diamonds." Cabin suites with fireplace. Weekly all-inclusive adult rates per person: $1,695(summer); $700-$1,290,(fall-spring).

IDAHO
Western Pleasure Guest Ranch ⊢

4675 Upper Gold Creek Road
Sandpoint, ID 83864
(208)263-9066
e-mail rschoonover@nidlink.com
Web: www.keokee.com/wpguestranch
Season: Year-round   Guest capacity: 20   Airport: Spokane, WA

Scenic Idaho Cowboy Adventures on a 3rd Generation Cattle Ranch.
Western Pleasure Guest Ranch is located 16 mi. NE of Sandpoint, Idaho. Guests can choose from modern hand-crafted log cabins, large enough to sleep eight, yet cozy enough for two, with fully furnished kitchens and wood stoves, or stay in our impressive 10,000 sq. ft. log lodge. It features six comfortable guest rooms, all with private baths, a large great room with a river rock fireplace, rec room, and loft area which is the perfect place to unwind with a good book.

NEW YORK
The Bark Eater Inn ⊢⊢🐴

Alstead Hill Rd. P.O. Box 139
Keene, NY 12942
(518)576-2221   (518) 576-2071 fax
e-mail: barkeater@trenet.com
Web: www.tvenet.com//barkeater
Season: Year-round   Guest capacity: 40   Airport: Albany, NY or Burlington, VT

Beginner or Old Hand...
this 19th century inn, set in a quiet Adirondack valley is for you. Trails and country roads beckon. Full size ring, instruction in English or western, and polo available. The Inn, carriage house and log cottage are filled with antiques. Full country breakfast included; gourmet dining by reservation. Olympic sites and cultural attractions are 15 minutes away in Lake Placid. Families welcome. Trailering encouraged. A true country inn. Livery and stable. Cross-country ski center.

WYOMING
Triple EEE Guest Ranch ⊢🐴

Rt. 287,   P.O. Box 538
Dubois, WY 82513
(800)353-2555 or (307)455-2304
e-mail: triplee@aol.com
Web: www.dudesville.com

Season: June - September   Guest capacity: 10
Airports: Jackson, WY or Riverton, WY

Western Fun for the Entire Family.
Located 80 miles from Yellowstone, this high mountain guest ranch offers the same majestic scenery as our nations most loved national park. Unlimited horseback riding takes you through the ruggedly beautiful Absaroka mountains. Help find and round-up cattle for shipment. Other activities include trout fishing, line dancing, western cookouts, sing alongs and much more. Cabins or lodge available.

COUNTRY INNS

Country Inns run the gamut of description from small personal Inns tucked away in country villages, to large country resorts. There is a high degree of personal involvement between the actual innkeepers and their guests. Many historic buildings have been utilized with furnishings reflecting the philosophies and enthusiasms of those innkeepers in meeting the historic preservation of their Inn. Each is different and embodies a quality of friendliness and welcome.

NEVADA
The Stonehouse Country Inn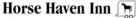
P.O. Box 77 or Hwy 290
Paradise Valley, NV 89426
(702)578-3530
Web: home.sprynet.com/sprynet/stonehouse.
Season: Year-round   Guest capacity: 18   Airport: Reno or Elko, NV

Truly A Trip To Paradise!
We have six spacious guest rooms with views from every room and large paddocks with shelter and safe fencing. Ride through the Santa Rosa Mountains and finish your day with a sumptuous meal surrounded by green lawns and blooming gardens. Reservations only, please.

NEW HAMPSHIRE
Horse Haven Inn
62 Raccoon Hill Road
Salisbury, NH 03268
(603)648-2101
Season: Year-round

Horses and Dogs are Welcomed At This "Country Comfortable" Inn
Sample the pleasures of a visit to a working farm where Thoroughbred foals frolic on the hillside. The 35 acre farm offers a tremendous view of surrounding mountains, quiet unpaved roads for carriage driving, and miles of riding and hiking trails. Enjoy an elaborate continental breakfast in the immense wood stoved kitchen, evening refreshments in the Carriage House "Gathering Room" and long days on the trail. Large bedded stalls or pipe corrals for horses. Off-leash romping for dogs.

NEW YORK
The Bark Eater Inn
Alstead Hill Rd.
P.O. Box 139
Keene, NY 12942
(518)576-2221   (518)576-2071 fax
e-mail: barkeater@trenet.com   Web: www.tvenet.com/barkeater.com
Season: Year-round   Guest capacity: 30
Airport: Albany, NY or Burlington, VT, pickup available

Beginner or Old Hand...
this 19th century inn set in a quiet Adirondack valley is for you. Trails and country roads beckon. Full size ring, instruction in English, western, and polo available. The Inn, carriage house and log cottage are filled with antiques. Full country breakfast included; gourmet dining by reservation. Olympic sites and cultural attractions are 15 minutes away in Lake Placid. Families welcome. Trailering encouraged. A true country inn, livery and stable. Winter: cross-country ski center.

TENNESSEE
Flintlock Farm
790 G'Fellers Road
Chuckey, TN 37641
(423) 257-2489
Season: Year-round   Guest capacity: 6
Airport: Tri-Cities, pickup available

Unforgettable Riding Adventures in the Land of Daniel Boone and Davy Crockett.
Come ride with us on beautiful Blue Ridge Mountain and valley trails. Create your own package combining unlimited riding with a wide variety of other outdoor activities. Spectacular mountain views from our lovingly restored and furnished 200 year old log cabin. We cater to small groups of experienced riders with warm southern hospitality, personal attention, cozy accommodations, country cooking, and the best of times!

VIRGINIA
Jordan Hollow Farm Inn
326 Hawksbill Park Road
Stanley, VA 22851
(540)778-2285 or
(888)418-7000 toll free
Web: www.jordanhollow.com
Season: Year-round
Guest capacity: 40
    except first 2 weeks in January
Airports: Dulles Int., Richmond, or
    Charlottesville, VA

A 200 Year Old Colonial Horse Farm.
A charming restored farmhouse with a wonderful restaurant featuring American Regional Cuisine. Twenty guest rooms, some featuring gas fireplaces, whirlpool tubs and TV's. Riding stable features leisurely 1 hour trail rides on our 145 acre farm and stalls for guest horses. Recommendations to other riding facilities in the area. Guide or maps for those bringing their horses. Group rates for 5 or more rooms. Located in serene Shenandoah Valley.

VIRGINIA
The Inn at
Meander Plantation
HCR 5, Box 460 A
Locust Dale, VA 22948
(800)385-4936
Season: Year-round   Guest capacity: 17-20
Airport: Charlottesville, or Dulles

Spectacular Colonial Country Inn in the Heart of Virginia's Hunt Country.
Grand colonial country estate, circa 1766, sits majestically on 80 acres of rolling hills and woods. Spectacular views of the Blue Ridge Mountains. Elegantly furnished rooms in major house and dependencies with private baths. Gourmet plantation breakfast served daily; other meals available. Horse boarding in on-premise stables. Enjoy riding, birdwatching, tubing on gentle Robinson River, walking nature trails. Between Washington D.C. and Charlottesville, Virginia near the Skyline Drive.

Dude Ranch Vacations
Make Memories

The dude ranch vacation is special. They are the perfect family destination, provide a place for singles to meld in with a group, and couples to make time for each other.

Each ranch is different showing the creative touches and interests of their owners to provide for a western theme. Ranches across the country range in size from small family operations to full scale resorts, each offering different programs. When you make inquiries about a ranch ask about their program. Some have very structured itineraries, with special activities for every day of the week. Others offer comfortable lodging, meals, and the opportunity to do what ever you wish, with horseback riding being the only scheduled activity.

They are the best family vacation available. Activities bring the whole family together doing things they probably wouldn't be able to do at home. Whether it's river rafting, jeep tours, square dancing, breakfast rides, chuckwagon suppers, fly fishing, gymkana, hiking, gold panning, swimming, boating, or a myriad of others, there is something for everyone. And of course, it is a dude ranch, there is always horseback riding.

Ask any grown up that vacationed at a dude ranch as a child what their fondest memories of childhood are and you will almost always find that dude ranch vacation mentioned, high up on the list! I still remember several ranch vacations from my childhood. All of the fun. And of course the names of all of my favorite ranch horses, Shorty, Fireball, Bucky, Hired Hand, Elvis... We returned to vacation with friends met while dude ranch vacationing, yearly. We looked forward to seeing the ranch family, they seemed like part of our family. How sad it was to leave them at the end of our week. But we could return the next year. We actually visited many ranches in different parts of the country. Along the way I have met guests that are back for their 25th year at the same place, bringing their children and grandchildren.

Try a dude ranch vacation this summer. Find out how special they really are, and make your own memories.

Who could forget Bucky
at the Painted Pony Ranch?

Symbols 🐴 Western riding 🐎 Take Your Own Horse Dude Ranch Association Members

DUDE & GUEST RANCHES

ALABAMA
Shady Grove Dude Ranch

P.O. Box 435
Mentone, AL 35984

(205)634-4344

Season: Year-round   Guest capacity: 45
Airport: Chattanooga, TN

**A Bit of Montana in Alabama,
We've Got It All!**
Atop lookout Mountain, find 100 miles of
scenic riding trails that include fishing lakes,
streams, deep forests, meadows, rocks,
caves, and waterfalls to enjoy. Horseback
or wagon rides. Ranch meals out on the
trail, hayrides, campfire stories, barn dances, swimming, rafting and fishing. Golf or skiing in season
at our own Cloudmont Ski and Golf Resort. Accommodation in lodges, bunkhouse or 5 bedroom
house for groups. Indoor and outdoor kitchens. Group rates.

ARIZONA
Bar BK Muleshoe Ranch

HC 37
Prescott, AZ 86301
(800)830-MULE (6853)   (310)831-9684 fax
e-mail: judybarbk@aol.com   Web: www.muleshoe-ranch.com
Season: Year-round   Guest capacity: 27   Weekly stays   Airport: Prescott or Phoenix

Wanted Cowboys & Cowgirls On Our Historic Cattle Ranch.
Experience life on a working cattle ranch. 28,000 acres of scenic Prescott, Arizona for you to ride.
Surrounded by beautiful terrain from waterfalls, rivers, and creeks to wide open, spacious desert.
We have quality accommodations and serve great food. We offer horseback riding, fishing, nature
walks, recreation room, exercise/weight room and much more. Near golf, museums, shopping,
concerts and theatre. For information or reservations call us or visit our website.

Visit
Arizona's
Oldest

Circle Z Ranch Working

Patagonia, Arizona 85624   Guest Ranch
1-888-854-5578

ARIZONA
Circle Z Ranch 🐎🤠
P.O. Box 194
Patagonia, AZ 85624
(888)854-2525 or (520)394-2525
(520) 394-2058 fax
e-mail: info@circlez.com
Web: www.circlez.com

Season: November 1 to May 15   Guest capacity: 40
Airport: Tucson, AZ, pickup available

Visit Arizona's Oldest Working Guest Ranch.
At an elevation of 4,000', you will ride ranch-bred horses through the historic Santa Rita and Patagonia mountains and across the ever-flowing Sonoita Creek. 6,000 acres, surrounded by National Forest afford adventurous half day and all day picnic rides, also a weekly overnight pack trip.
Stay in attractively furnished adobe cottages; tennis court, heated pool, hiking trails. You'll love our excellent food and down-home hospitality during your stay.

ARIZONA
Flying E Guest Ranch 🐎🐴🤠
2801 W. Wickenburg Way
Wickenburg, AZ 85390
(520)684-2690   (520)684-5304 fax
e-mail: flyinge@primenet.comWeb: www.duderanch.org

Season: November 1 to May 1   Guest capacity: 32   Airport: Phoenix, AZ

We Are Arizona's "Riding Ranch"!
Particular care is given by our barn staff to pair people with horses for riding enjoyment of our 20,000 acres of beautiful hi-desert country. High on a mesa at 2700'...Flying E offers the best of food, served family style, comfortable, immaculate accommodations, pool/hot spa, tennis and exercise room plus horse related activities...a world all its own. See our ranch in color on page 7.

ARIZONA
Grapevine Canyon Ranch
P.O. Box 302
Pearce, AZ 85625   🐎🤠
(800)245-9202 or (520)826-3185
(520) 826-3636 fax
e-mail: egrapevine@earthlink.net
Web: www.gcranch.com

Season: Year-round   Guest capacity: 30
Airport: Tucson, AZ, pickup available

Desert Hospitality for Adults.
A working guest ranch in Arizona's beautiful high desert. You will enjoy comfortable, secluded accommodations. Our guests participate in daily riding through spectacular mountain country. Seasonal cattle work for experienced riders. At meal times, delicious country-style meals will pique your appetite. Walk-trot-canter riding. We cater to adults, no children under 12 please.

ARIZONA
The Horseshoe Ranch
on Bloody Basin Road
HCR 34, Box 5005
Mayer, AZ 86333
(520)632-8813
e-mail: hranch@primenet.com
Web: www.primenet.com/~hranch/
Season: September - June
Guest capacity: 12   Airport: Phoenix, AZ

Ride For the Horseshoe Brand.
Experienced riders come to do what they have never done before – work cattle from the saddle of a cattle-savvy ranch horse. Riders find doing real cowboy work the "Ultimate High". 70,000 acres of mesas, canyons and mountains in snow-free Arizona. Saddle up and do what needs done for the day, sorting, searching for strays, gathering, driving, roping, riding fence, branding and doctoring. Then shower off the trail dust in your own private ranch house room and enjoy a hearty ranch meal.

ARIZONA
Kay El Bar Guest Ranch
P.O. Box 2480
Wickenburg, AZ 85358
(800)684-7583 or (520)684-7593 (520)684-4497 fax
e-mail: kelbar@juno.com   Web: www.kayelbar.com
Season: Mid-October - May   Guest capacity: 24   Airport: Phoenix, AZ

Come to Sunny Arizona, Visit an Old Fashioned Dude Ranch – A National Historic Site.
Located in the foothills of the Bradshaw Mountains on the Hassayampa River, the Kay El Bar Ranch offers some of the finest horseback riding in the Mid-Sonoran Desert. Walk-trot-canter riding. The old adobe buildings and comfortable accommodations maintain the casual atmosphere of a real dude ranch vacation. You will find excellent, plentiful meals, a heated pool and yard games to complete the scene. Trail riding for guests age 7 and up. Limited stabling for private horses.

ARIZONA
Lazy K Bar Ranch
8401 N. Scenic Drive
Tucson, AZ 85743
(800)321-7018 or (520) 744-3050
e-mail: lazyk@theriver.com
Web: www.guestranches.com/lazykbar
Season: Mid-September - Mid-June
Airport: Tucson, AZ   Guest capacity: 50

**Enjoy Home Cooking, Horseback Riding,
and a Relaxed Atmosphere.**
Well-known for its friendly staff, the Lazy K Bar Ranch has been serving its own brand of Western hospitality since 1936. All of our 23 comfortable, southwestern style rooms have a private bath and air conditioning. Our riding program is geared to individual ability. Swimming, tennis, hiking, biking, hayrides, trap shooting, horse shoes, volleyball, shuffleboards and cookouts are also available.

ARIZONA
Merv Griffin's
Wickenburg Inn & Dude Ranch 🐴

34801 N Highway 89
Wickenburg, AZ 85390
(800)942-5362 or (520)684-7811
(520) 684-2981 fax
Web: www.merv.com

Season: Year-round   Guest capacity: 150   Airport: Phoenix, AZ

This is Where the Pavement Ends and the Adventure Begins!
Our warm, western hospitality includes desert trail rides, cattle drives, cookouts, riding lessons, all-day rides, roping lessons, swimming, arts & crafts, nature hikes and mountain bikes. Three pools, two hot tubs, 54 charming hillside casitas and 9 lodge rooms. Children's program available during Holidays and Spring Break for a family vacation they'll always remember! Ask about the Romance package, Cowgirl Camp and Educational Workshops. See page 3.

ARIZONA
Rancho de la Osa 🐴

P.O. Box 1
Sasabe, AZ 85633-0001
(800)872-6240 or (520)823-4257
Web: osagal@aol.com

Season: Year-round   Guest capacity: 43   Airport: Tucson, AZ

Visit One of the Last Great Spanish Haciendas Built in the 1700's.
The Spanish settlers called it: "Ranch of the She Bear", which has been modernized as a place of superb lodging for our guests. Adobe guest rooms surround a spacious courtyard. Located in the high Sonoran Desert, in the shadow of Baboquivari Peak, you will find marvelous riding from 2 hours to a full day on either walk-trot, or loping rides. Enjoy a ride to the Buenos Aires National Wildlife Refuge or Presumido Trading Post then return for a dip in the pool or hot tub. Superb southwestern meals.

ARIZONA
White Stallion Ranch 🐴🤠

9251 West Twin Peaks Road
Tucson, AZ 85743
(888)977-2624   (520)744-2786 fax
Web: www.wsranch.com

Season: September-June   Guest capacity: 75   Airport: Tucson, AZ , pickup available

Close to Civilization and Yet So Far Away.
Escape the city to find fresh air, sunshine and relax. Owned and operated by the True family for 34 years. Extensive riding on horses chosen just for you on our 3,000 acre ranch and neighboring Saguaro National Park. Heated pool, tennis, hot tub, petting zoo, weekly rodeos, breakfast rides, hayrides, nature walks, steak barbecues. We offer 4 rides per day, both slow and fast or all day over gorgeous mountain and desert trails. Just 17 miles from Tucson, find the Old Southwest.

🐴 Western Riding   🐴 English Riding   🐴 Take Your Own Horse   🐴 Dude Ranch Association Members

ARKANSAS
Scott Valley Resort and Guest Ranch ⛑🏇

Box 1447-HL
Mountain Home, AR 72653
(870) 425-5136   Web: www.scottvalley.com
Season: Year-round   Guest capacity: 65   Airport: Springfield, MO or Little Rock, AR

Missouri Foxtrotters For Your Riding Pleasure!
Whether you are an experienced rider or novice, the Cooper's have placed quality horseback riding as a priority on their ranch. These are "homegrown" superb horses, YOU actually get to ride! Rides are commensurate to ability, and we have one just right for you! Nestled in the Ozark Mountains, you get all the beautiful scenery without the concern of altitude sickness. Summer is aimed at Family fun, lots of it. Spring and fall are geared for the serious rider who wants lots of time in the saddle. (Ask about our All Adult Week.)

CALIFORNIA
Alisal Guest Ranch ⛑

1054 Alisal Road
Solvang, CA 93463
(800)425-4725 or (805)688-6411   e-mail: info@alisal.com   Web: www.alisal.com
Season: Year-round   Airport: Santa Barbara, CA   Guest capacity: 200

Journey Back to the Old West.
Find 10,000 acres of scenic trails for riders of all levels. Saddle up with our experienced wranglers for a breakfast ride to an historic adobe camp. Gallop through oak-shaded valleys to our private lake. Venture out with your own guide to explore the quiet grandeur of our wide open spaces. Special children's riding program. Rodeos for groups. Two 18-hole golf courses.

CALIFORNIA
Coffee Creek Ranch ⛑🏇

HC 2, Box 4940 - RV
Trinity Center, CA 96091
(800)624-4480 or (530) 266-3343 (530)266-3597 fax
Web: www.coffeecreekranch.com
Season: Year-round   Airport: Redding, CA   Guest capacity: 50

Northern California's Finest Guest Ranch. Rated AAA 3-Diamond.
Enjoy a wonderful family horseback vacation in scenic California. See our ad to the right, for a list of the many activities which we offer. Then join us for fun and relaxation. ADA accessible.

CALIFORNIA
Hunewill
Guest Ranch ⛑🏇

P.O. Box 368 HL
Bridgeport, CA 93517
(760)932-7710   (760)932-7933 fax   Web: www.hunewillranch.com
Season: May - Late September   Guest capacity: 45   Airport: Reno, NV

**Hunewill Ranch – A Family Owned & Operated Working Cattle Ranch Since 1861.
You won't want to go home!**
Horseback riding is our specialty. 130 horses, one just right for you. Children's riding program, breathtaking mountain scenery. Hay rides, dancing, cattle work, Fall Color Ride, 5 day Cattle Drive and more. **Free color brochure.**

CANADA – Alberta
Black Cat
Guest Ranch
Box 6267
Hinton, AB, Canada T7V 1X6
(403) 865-3084 (403)865-1924 fax
e-mail:bcranch@agt.net
Web: www.agt.net/public/bcranch/
Season may 15 to October 15
Guest capacity: 35
Airport: Edmonton International

Your Vacation Dollar Goes Further in Canada.
Tucked away in a beautiful valley of the Canadian Rocky Mountains, our lodge has just 16 guest rooms - you won't find a crowd here, but a friendly group of fellow travellers and our Black Cat staff. Enjoy scenic trail riding and hiking on many miles of varied trails. Hike, raft, line dancing. Special events – Spa Weekends, Murder Mysteries, Guided Hikes, Cave trips, Art and Writing Workshops, Elderhostel. For great sight-seeing, we're only one hour's drive away from Jasper.

CANADA – Alberta
Brewster's Kananaskis
Guest Ranch
P.O. Box 964
Banff, AB, Canada, T0L 0C0
(800)691-5085 or (403)673-3737
(403)673-2100 fax

Season: May to September   Guest capacity: 60   Airport: Calgary, AB

Historic Guest Ranch Set in the Spectacular Beauty of the Canadian Rockies.
Providing wonderful vacations since 1923. Our cabin and chalet units feature antique furnishings and cedar interiors for groups or individuals. We specialize in horseback riding, overnight pack trips, western barbecues, and gala events with entertainment, licensed dining room and lounge. Also enjoy our whirlpool, and river rafting. An ideal retreat-style conference location, private meeting rooms available.

CANADA – British Columbia
Chilcotin Holidays 🐎
Guest Ranch

Gun Creek Road
Gold Bridge, BC Canada V0K 1P0
(250)238-2274 phone/fax
e-mail: chilcotinholidays@bc.sympatico.ca
Web: www.chilcotinholidays.com

Season: Year-round   Guest capacity: 16
Airport: Vancouver International,
          pickup available: Chilcotin Express

Four Seasons of Wilderness Adventures in the Sunny South Chilcotin Mountains.
Novice and advanced riders enjoy sure-footed mountain cayuse horses with licensed guides at our spacious guest ranch with 2 story fireplace or in our permanent alpine base camps with log cabins, gravity fed hot showers and tent cabins with heaters, throughout our 2,000 sq. mile outfitting area. Our 7 distinct adventures include: guest ranch stays, wildlife viewing pack trips, guide training, fly-in fishing, hiking, biking, and winter adventures. Located just 4-1/2 hours north of Vancouver.

CANADA – British Columbia
Three Bars Cattle 🐎
& Guest Ranch

SS 3, Site 19-62
Cranbrook, BC V1C 6H3 Canada
(250) 426-5230
email: threebarsranch@cyberlink.ca.baWeb: www.threebarsranch.com
Season: May-September   Guest capacity: 40   Airport: Cranbrook, via Calgary or Vancouver

Experience the Canadian West Three Bars Style. In the heart of the Canadian Rockies.
Vacations on a working cattle ranch in upscale accommodations. Riding is the main activity, with 60-70 horses, we can fit horses to your riding ability. Arena instruction time included, trail riding, and weekly team penning competition. Activities include, river rafting, fly-fishing and guided hiking. Ranch facilities include new log cabins, log lodge, indoor heated pool, hot tub, tennis court, volley ball, horseshoes and fire pit for evening gatherings. Great Meals, friendly staff and fantastic scenery.

COLORADO
American Safari Ranch

P.O. Box 128
Fairplay, CO 80440 🐎
(719) 836-2431
Fax request: 888-551-4710
Season: May - October
Guest capacity: 75   Airport: Denver, CO

Our Main Emphasis is on the Quality of Our Horses and Riding.
Exceptional riding on a Rocky Mountain ranch in central Colorado. No nose to tail here. Ride like a cowboy over our spectacular 3,500 acre ranch. Guided, unguided, riding lessons or private rides with your personal wrangler. Programs for beginners to expert riders. Modern luxury log cabins or lodge rooms with private bath. Hearty western style food and BBQ, prepared right here on the ranch kitchen. Something for everyone, riding, rafting, fishing, hayrides, golf driving range, hiking etc.

COLORADO
Aspen Canyon Ranch

13206 County Road 3, Star Route
Parshall, CO 80468
1-800-321-1357
Season: May to October   Guest capacity: 24
Airport: Denver, CO

Enter Into The Old West!
Cross Ute Pass, view the snow-capped Gore
Range, and enter the famous Williams Fork
Valley. Our small mountain ranch, blends
magnificent scenery, privacy and comfortable facilities with Old Colorado flavor. Luxurious log cabins set overhanging the river. Ride long days on our ranch, work cattle, or trailer to a variety of trailheads. Many riding options including barrel racing and roping in our arena. Deluxe western cuisine with a gourmet touch. Relax in the hot tub, watch the river rush by gaze at the mountains. Enjoy fishing, hiking and good friends.

COLORADO
Aspen Lodge at Estes Park

6120 Hwy 7
Estes Park, CO 80517
(800)332-MTNS or (970) 586-8133
Web: www.aspenlodge.com
Season: Year-round   Guest capacity: 180
Airport: Denver, CO

**Fulfill Your Western Dreams
at Aspen Lodge.**
Superb accommodations in the largest log lodge in Colorado or in our cabins. Enjoy trail riding on our 3,000 acre working ranch and at our resort adjoining Rocky Mountain National Park with novice to advanced riding programs. Multitude of activities on property including swimming, fishing, hiking, mountain bikes and more, plus extensive winter activities.

COLORADO
Bar Lazy J Guest Ranch

Box N
Parshall, CO 80468
(800)396-6279 or (970)725-3437
e-mail: barlazyj@rkymtnhi.com
Web: www.barlazyj.com
Season: May-October Guest capacity: 38
Airport: Denver, CO

**Colorado's Oldest,
Continuously Operating Guest Ranch.**
Nestled in a peaceful valley along the beau-
tiful Colorado river. GOLD MEDAL fishing.
Scenic horseback riding - all levels. Walk-trot-lope rides. Breakfast and all-day rides. Warm Western hospitality; delicious home cooking served in our historic lodge. Children's program, evening entertainment, recreation barn, swimming pool / jacuzzi. Listen to the river rush by just outside your private log cabin.

COLORADO
Buffalo Horn Ranch 🐴

13825 County Rd. 7
Meeker, CO 81641
(970)878-5450   (970)878-4088 fax
Web: www.buffalohorn.com
Season: May - September   Guest capacity: 25+
Airport: Grand Junction, CO

This is Cowboy Country!
Sagebrush dotted mountainsides and wide open
spaces at 6,500 feet! Swing into the saddle, ride,
rope, drive cattle. Take in magnificent views, breathe in fresh high country air, fish the White River
or shoot some clays. Breakfast hearty, lunch on the trail, chow down at a BBQ and dine in gourmet
style! Adventure in the great outdoors and then enjoy the creature comforts of our spacious lodge
and our gracious accommodations. Treat yourself to rural grandeur, Western style.

COLORADO
C Lazy U Ranch 🤠

P.O. Box 379
Granby, CO 80446
(970)887-3344   (970)887-3917 fax
e-mail: ranch@clazyu.com
Web: www.clazyu.com
Season: Summer June-Oct.
Winter Dec.-March   Guest capacity: 110
Airport: Denver, CO

Summer Brings a Full Riding Program for All Riding Levels.
A Mobil 5-Star, AAA 5-Diamond guest ranch. Open summer and winter. Fast, medium and slow rides
for different abilities. Morning afternoon and weekly picnic rides. Separate rides for children and
adults. Buck Brannaman horsemanship clinic in the Fall. Some adults only weeks. Winter sleigh
rides. Join us while we feed our herd of 150 with our team. Winter, take to the trails in the snow or
ride in our indoor arena. Fully supervised children's program, ages 3 and up. Walk-trot-lope.

COLORADO
Colorado Trails Ranch 🤠

12161-B County Road 240
Durango, CO 81301
(800)323-DUDE (3833)
or (970) 247-5055   (970) 385-7372 fax
e-mail:CoTRanch@aol
Web: www.colotrails.com
Season: Late May-Early October
Guest capacity: 65   Airport: Durango, CO

Ride Into the Romance of the Old West.
Imagine riding along a mountain stream under
a canopy of Aspen and Pine trees. Your partner is a horse perfectly matched to your riding ability.
Enjoy our cozy mountain cabins, delicious home cooked meals and western hospitality. Other
activities include fly-fishing, shooting sports, water skiing, hiking, hayrides, cookouts and evening
entertainment. Excellent children/teen program

COLORADO
Coulter Lake Guest Ranch
0080 County Rd. 273
P.O. Box 906
Rifle, CO 81650
(800)858-3046 (970)625-1473 fax
e-mail: coulterlake@webtv.net
Web: www.guestranches.com/coulterlake

Season: Memorial Day to Sept. 30
Guest capacity: 30
Airport: Grand Junction, CO, pickup avail.

Remote Old West Mountain Ranch on a Spectacular Lake!
Since 1936, our small size has allowed each guest to be special. Our spectacular White River National Forest setting offers trails through wildflowers, aspen and spruce, unchanged since Indian times. Beautiful private lake for swimming, fishing, or boating. See elk and deer. Ride good mountain trail horses. Enjoy homestyle cooking and cozy log cabins nestled by the lake or among trees.

COLORADO
Drowsy Water Ranch
P.O. Box 147-RV
Granby, CO 80446
(970)725-3456 Reservations (800)845-2292

e-mail: dwrken@aol.com

Season: June 7-September 12
Airport: Denver, CO
Guest capacity: 60

We Offer the Complete Horse Program.
Fast, slow, all day, instruction and cookout rides. Your own horse for the week at our secluded ranch. We have a supervised children's program, 5 and under and 6 - 13 yr. olds. Enjoy our recently remodelled log cabin or lodge accommodations. Lots of evening activities including hayrides, square dance, carnivals, and more.

COLORADO
Harmel's Ranch Resort
P.O. Box 399
Almont, CO 81210
(800)235-3402 or (970)641-1740
email: harmels@gunnison.com
Web: www.coloradovacation.com/duderanch/harmels

Season: Mid-May - September   Airport: Gunnison, CO   Guest capacity: 120

A Family Mountain Guest Ranch - - and a Whole Lot More!
Stay a few days or an entire week amidst the tree lined rivers in beautiful Taylor Creek Canyon enjoying horseback rides through spectacular mountain wilderness, whitewater rafting, mountain bicycling, hayrides, chuckwagon cookouts, square dances, children's program, kid's fishing pond, swimming pool and evening entertainment. Enjoy riverside dining. From hearty steak eaters to vegetarians, our entrees will tantalize all, complemented by homemade soups, breads and desserts.

COLORADO
Latigo Ranch
Box 237
Kremmling, CO 80459
(970)724-9008
e-mail: latigo@compuserve.com

Season: June to October
Guest capacity: 35
Airport: Denver, CO

Like Family Comin' Home.
Noted for its top-notch wranglers and staff,
Latigo's unbeatable riding program helps novice or advanced riders improve their horsemanship. Walk, trot, lope, all-day, overnight, sunset and breakfast rides on 200 miles of trails through meadows, up peaks, along gurgling mountain streams or Aspen groves. Whether working cattle or flyfishing, families with kids love Latigo. Scrumptions meals, inviting cabins.

COLORADO
Lost Valley Ranch
29555 Goose Creek Road, Box HL
Sedalia, CO 80135
(303)647-2311   (303)647-2315 fax
e-mail: lostranch@aol.com
Web: www.ranchweb.com/lost

Season: March 1-December 1
Guest capacity: 95
Airport: Denver or Colorado Springs, CO

Discover Our Year-'round Authentic Working Cattle/Horse Ranch.
Just 80 miles from Denver or Colorado Springs. Blaze new trails while exploring 26,000 acres of the Rocky Mountains. We have year 'round riding, cattle roundups, special horsemanship weeks, weekly rodeos and an Orvis fly-fishing school. AAA rated "4 Diamonds." Cabin suites with fireplace. Weekly all-inclusive adult rates per person: $1,695(summer); $700-$1,290,(fall-spring).

COLORADO
Mountain Meadows
Guest Ranch

237 County Road 48
Gunnison, CO 81230
(970)641-9501

Season: Year-round   Airport: Gunnison, CO

Capture a Moment Out of Time...at Mountain Meadows.
A riding retreat for the most serious horseman to the weekend enthusiast. Experienced trainers available to instruct English and Western. School over our cross-country course, indoor and outdoor arenas. Ride out over miles and miles of breathtaking trail. Enjoy an overnight pack trip. Rooms are charming. Rates are modest. And the area's great for every kind of outdoor activity you can possibly wish for. Fly-fishing, hiking, mountain biking, white water rafting, great BBQ's, vacation packages.

COLORADO
Old Glendevey Ranch

Glendevey Colorado Route
3219 County Rd. 190
Jelm, WY 82063
(800)807-1444
e-mail: glendevey@aol.com
Web: www.duderanch.org/glendevey

Season: May to November
Guest capacity: 18
Airport: Laramie, WY   Weekly stays

A True Wilderness Experience.
We are a small family run guest ranch that offers a charming, warm setting with all the traditional activities of a guest ranch. We "specialize" in saddle horse and pack mule pack trips to our 10,000' Rawah Wilderness base camp. There you may fish the high lakes & beaver ponds, ride and enjoy the surrounding beauty. "A wonderful way to rough it."

COLORADO
Powderhorn Guest Ranch

1525 County Road 27
Powderhorn, CO 81243
(970)641-0220
(800)786-1220
e-mail: powguest@rmi.net
Web: www.powderhornguestranch.com

Season: May 30- September 12
Guest Capacity: 30   Weekly stays
Airport: Gunnison, CO, pickup, available

Join us for a Relaxing, Fun-Filled Vacation!
Enjoy a friendly family atmosphere at our secluded ranch in the Powderhorn Valley near Gunnison, Colorado. Scenic horseback rides in the Powderhorn Primitive Area adjacent to the ranch, as well as instruction and schooling in our arena. All-inclusive American plan with delicious home-cooked meals served in our log lodge with fireplaces and game tables or on the river-side picnic island. Carpeted log cabins, great fishing, heated swimming pool, and hot tub. Wonderful family destination.

COLORADO
Rawah Ranch 🐴

Summer

Glendevey, Colorado Rt.	Winter
11447 N County Road 103	1612 Adriel Circle
Jelm, WY 82063	Ft. Collins, CO 80524

(800)820-3152 or (970)484-8288 or (970)435-5715
e-mail: rawah@compuserve.com
Season: June-September   Guest capacity: 34
Airport: Laramie, WY, pickup, available

**Rawah Ranch is Known as
THE RIDING RANCH for Serious Trail Riders.**
Talk about escape! We're talking moose, elk, deer, coyotes, pronghorn, wildflowers, Everywhere! Snowcaps. Waterfalls. Wilderness. Stunning, secluded valley. Imagine RIDING your "own" fine Rawah horse **YOUR WAY**– high -snowfields, **low** -ghost ranches, **fast** - sage meadows, **slow** - breathtaking overlooks, alpine lakes. All day, any day. Beautiful log cabins. Private baths. Fireplaces. Porches. Hot tub. "Too good" food. "Just right" evening programs.

COLORADO
Sylvan Dale Guest Ranch 🐴

2939 N. County Road 31 D
Loveland, CO 80538
(970)667-3915   (970)635-9336 fax
e-mail: ranch@sylvandale.com
Web: www.sylvandale.com

Season: Year-round Guest capacity: 65 Airport: Denver, CO

Discover Your Inner Cowboy!
The Jessup family welcomes you to their 3,000 acre historic ranch. Enjoy overnight pack trips, gymkhana, our great horsemanship program, and walk-trot-lope trail rides. Ranch raised Quarter horses. Western cookouts, superb fly-fishing, swimming, tennis, children's program, and Mrs. Jessup's delicious home-baking! Family entertainment each

evening. Golf, rafting and Rocky Mountain National Park nearby. 6 nights lodging in comfortable country accommodations. Great for family reunions! Adults Only Week, end of August. Conveniently located one hour from Denver. Dude ranching since 1946.

COLORADO
Waunita Hot Springs Ranch 🐴

8007 County Road 887, Box 7L
Gunnison, CO 81230
(970) 641-1266

Season: June-September   Airport: Gunnison, CO   Guest capacity: 50

Enjoy Beautiful Scenery, History and the Soothing Waters of Waunita Hot Springs.
Sharing our 35th year with families, couples and singles seeking a wholesome, no alcohol vacation atmosphere. Trail rides grouped by age and ability or families may ride together...from flowered meadows to snow-ridged mountain tops. Fishing, cookouts, overnight campout, musical show, 4X4 trips, and rafting. Relax in our unique hot springs pool, enjoy comfortable accommodations and yummy meals. Reasonable, all-inclusive rates.

COLORADO
Wilderness Trails Ranch 🐎

1776 County Road 302
Durango, CO 81301
(800)527-2624 or (970)247-0722
e-mail:wtr@sprynet.com Web: www.wildernesstrails.com
Season: May 31-October 4
Guest capacity: 48   Airport: Durango, CO

A Unique Blend of the Past and Present.
Satisfy your senses. Coyotes sing. Air invigorates. Brilliant stars captivate. Warm hellos. Difficult goodbyes. Well appointed log cabins. Wide menu of riding by skill level. Visit our foals. Children's programs for ages 3-17, for never-bored kids. Pool, hot tub, fishing, water skiing, rafting, Mesa Verde Cliff Dwellings, Narrow Gauge Railroad, 4-WD trips. Fun evenings: campfire singalong, hayrides, staff show, country dances and lessons, relax! All inclusive rates--no gratuities. September Adults only & cattle roundup. Featured on "Good Morning America" and PBS Special "Going Places".

COLORADO
Wind River Ranch 🐎

P.O. Box 3410
Estes Park, CO 80517
(970)586-4212 (970)586-2255 fax
e-mail: wolff@windriverranch.com
Web: www.windriverranch.com
Season: June to Sept. Guest capacity: 50 Airport: Denver, CO

A Vacation With a Purpose.
Wind River is a Christian family guest ranch. Trail rides into the Rocky Mountain National Park as well as Roosevelt National Forest. Located in the magnificent Tahosa Valley at 9,200 feet with spectacular views of Long's Peak. Variety of rides to accommodate the skills of each rider. Wrangler breakfast, steak cook out, and hayrides for the entire family. Kids program also available.

COLORADO
Wit's End Guest Ranch & Resort 🐎

254 County Road 500
Bayfield, CO 81122
(970) 884-4113
Season: Year-round   Airport: Durango, LaPlata   Guest capacity: 80

Historic Wit's End Ranch, Founded in 1859.
Situated in a narrow valley surrounded by 12,000 and 14,000 ft. peaks adjacent to Vallecito Lake (6 miles long). Luxury class log cabins and fine dining in our 125 year old lodge. Enjoy mountain, lake and high country riding with our 100 horses, rodeo arena, full children's program, pack trips, horse and cattle drives, fly-fishing, 50' heated pool, hot tubs, tennis, biking, guided hiking, 4-wheel drive trips. Winter, cross country skiing, snow trail on horseback, snowmobiling, pond skating and sleigh rides. Ranked as one of the country's 12 best by Country Inns Magazine and featured in Elegant Hotels. Please see color photos on pages 4 and 5.

IDAHO
Moose Creek Ranch 🐴🤠

P.O. Box 350
Victor, ID 83455
1-800-676-0075 or (208) 787-2784
e-mail: moosecreekranch@pdt.net
Web: www.webfactor.com/mooscrk/

Season: June 1- September 30
Guest capacity: 35
Airport: Jackson, WY, pickup available

**Breathtaking Rides Await You
in the Heart of the
Majestic Teton Mountains.**

Seasoned wranglers provide personal guidance to experienced and beginning riders. Little tykes have their own programs and day care. Other activities include square dancing, an evening at a western show and a raft trip on the Snake River. Variety of accommodations/all ages welcome. Homecooked family style meals served in the main lodge or outdoors. Indoor heated pool, sauna and hot tub round out our comfortable relaxed mountain home. Yellowstone 1-1/2 hours drive and the night life and shopping of Jackson Hole, Wyoming only 30 minutes away.

IDAHO
Western Pleasure Guest Ranch 🐴

4675 Upper Gold Creek Road
Sandpoint, ID 83864
(208)263-9066
e-mail rschooonover@nidlink.com
Web: www.keokee.com/wpguestranch

Season: Year-round   Guest capacity: 20   Airport: Spokane, WA

Scenic Idaho, Breathtaking Mountain Views!
Western Pleasure Guest Ranch is located 16 miles N.E. of Sandpoint, Idaho on a 3rd generation cattle ranch. Guests at the ranch can choose from modern hand-crafted log cabins, or enjoy a cozy room in the new lodge. You will ride among tall pines and enjoy breathtaking views of the Selkirk and Cabinet Mountain Ranges. Your hosts, Roley and Janice Schoonover, would love to show you around the ranch on horseback, by buggy or during winter, sleigh. Winter also brings cross-country skiing.

LOUISIANA
St John Ranch 🐴🐴

St. John Rd, Route 1, Box 109
Homer, LA 71040
(318)927-4484

Season: Year-round   Guest capacity: 60
Airport: Shreveport, LA

**We Specialize in Riding Vacations,
Retreats, Seminars and Reunions.**
Come ride our rolling hills on a great
horse. Located in northern Louisiana, we provide 3 great meals daily, comfortable lodging, a heated pool, golf nearby and miles of trails over varied terrain. Over 2,000 beautiful acres of rolling hills and private lakes. Our lakes offer scenic beauty as well as fishing and boating. Singles, families, and groups are welcome.

MEXICO
Rancho del Oso
Cerocahui, Chihuahua, Mexico
U.S. representative: Native Trails
613 Queretaro
El Paso, TX 79912-2210
(800)884-3107   (915)833-3107

Season: October-April
Guest capacity: 6
Airports: Los Mochis or Chihuahua

Copper Canyon --
Where Horses Climb Mountains.
Our Batopilas run is an adventure package pushing the limits of mountain riding. Covers 150 miles of rugged mountain trail with elevation changes totaling over 8 miles. The ride starts in Cerocahui, descends to the canyon bottom, gold mining pueblo of Urique, crosses high mountains to the legendary silver mining capitol of Batopilas, has a day for resting and exploring, then return over different trails. Or stay at our comfortable ranch and enjoy day rides. 5-8 hours of riding per day.

MICHIGAN
Double JJ
Resort Ranch
P.O. Box 94
Rothbury, MI 49452
(616) 894-4444
e-mail: info@doublejjj.com

Season: Year-round
Guest capacity: 250
Airport: Muskegon, MI

Enjoy the Best of the West in Western Michigan!
Our 1,500 wooded acres provide excellent riding vacations. All-inclusive packages include ranch style lodging, 3 meals daily, beginner to advanced rides for different types of riders, breakfast and steak rides, rodeo, entertainment, D.J's & live bands, target sports, swimming pool & spa, boating, fishing, mini-golf, and volleyball. Tee off at our Thoroughbred Golf Club, a championship, 18 hole course designed by Arthur Hills.

MICHIGAN
El Rancho Stevens, Inc.
2332 E. Dixon Lake Road
P.O. Box 495
Gaylord, MI 49735
(517)732-5090

Season: May 24-September 29   Guest capacity: 85   Airport: Traverse City, MI

Northern Michigan's Best Kept Secret.
Located 5 miles S.E. of Gaylord, Michigan, El Rancho Stevens is an excellent family destination, resort-ranch. We cater to the family with every activity imaginable, horseback riding, water skiing, boating, swimming (in lake or heated pool), hay rides, dancing, corral games, indoor riding arena and children's program. Special rates for groups. Golf nearby.

MICHIGAN
Wolf Lake Ranch Resort, Inc. 🐴
Rt 2, Box 2514
Baldwin, MI 49304
(616)745-3890

Season: April 19-November 3   Guest capacity: 65   Airport: Baldwin, MI

Family Guest Ranch in the Middle of the Manistee National Forest.
Wolf Lake Ranch is considered a riders paradise...Ride horseback on old logging roads, following miles of trails. Imagine the unexpected thrill of discovering wildlife in their natural habitat. After your ride you'll find activities galore! Something for everyone. Swim in crystal-clear, sand bottom Wolf Lake. Play tennis, volleyball, shuffleboard, basketball, ping pong, boating, fishing, horseshoes, and dancing, take a hayride under the star-studded sky or just relax at a campfire. Soak in the jacuzzi or play golf nearby. Enjoy three family style meals a day.

MISSOURI
Bucks & Spurs Guest Ranch 🐴
Rt. 4, Box 740
Ava, MO 65608
(417)683-2381
Web: www.bucksandspurs.com

Season: Year round   Guest capacity: 30   Airport: Springfield, MO

Saddle Up and Ride Back in Time, on a Secluded, 1,000 Acres, Not Far From Branson.
A real working ranch offering a blend of western charm and history. Refreshing, exhilarating riding for all levels. Not just head to tail walking. Ride through forests, freshly mowed hayfields, along Big Beaver Creek. Canoe or fish for abundant brown bass. Catch a glimpse of deer, beaver, or wild turkeys. Explore the remains of Fort Lawrence, a Union, Civil War fort or hunt for arrowheads where the Osage and Cherokee once lived. Comfortable, newly remodeled lodging and excellent meals.

MONTANA
Blacktail Ranch 🐴
4440 South Fork Trail
Wolf Creek, MT 59648
(406)235-4330
Guest capacity: 30
Airport: Great Falls, MT, pickup available

Spectacular Mountain Working Guest Ranch.
Family owned and operated for over 100 years. We have it all! Unlimited riding on a great string of Paint horses in some of Montana's most beautiful mountains. Over-night trail rides across the Continental Di-  vide - Cattle Drives all season - Abundant Wildlife and Wild Flowers - Hiking Trails - 8 miles of Private Trout Stream - Day trips on the Missouri River and numerous Native American Sites. We also boast newly renovated cabins exceptional home cooking, hot tub and sauna. Western hospitality on a real Montana ranch.

Travel tip: Want to take your saddle along? Get one of the heavy canvas saddle carriers, available by catalog or tack shop. Place a small duffel bag filled with your riding apparel, boots, jeans, slicker... in the bottom for use as a saddle rack. Put your saddle in over this to help protect the tree.

MONTANA
JJJ Wilderness Ranch
Box 310 - R
Augusta, MT 59410
(406)562-3653   (406)562-3836 fax
e-mail:triplej@3rivers.net
Web: www.triplejranch.com

Season: June 1-September 30 Guest Capacity: 20
Airport: Great Falls, MT , pickup available

Hospitality- a WesternTradition We Come By Naturally.
The Barker family has shared this western tradition for over 2 decades. Located above the beautiful Sun River Canyon and Gibson Lake, the JJJ specializes in family vacations emphasizing horseback riding, trout fishing and hiking. Our Kiddie Wrangler supervises fun rides & games. Traditional cowboy steak barbecues, an overnight pack-trip, simple mountain climbing, swimming, and evening firesides of cowboy poetry and tale telling. Fully outfitted horseback trips into the famous Bob Marshall Wilderness. Providing an ultimate outdoor vacation experience is our goal!

MONTANA
Lake Upsata Guest Ranch
Box 6, 135 Lake Upsata Road
Ovando, MT 59854
(800)594-7687 or (406)793-5890
e-mail: rhowe@upsata.com   Web:www.upsata.com

Season: May-September   Guest capacity: 40   Airport Missoula, MT

There's Something for Everyone!!!
Located on a spectacular mountain lake in Western Montana. Private lakeside cabins, homecooked meals, FLY FISHING instruction on blue ribbon trout rivers, HORSEBACK RIDING through the Northern Rockies, and CHILDREN'S PROGRAMS. Plus swimming, canoeing, campfires, barbecues, boating, kayaking, hiking, tubing down the river, mountain biking, tours to ghost towns, and more.

MONTANA
Lazy EL Ranch
P.O. Box 90
Roscoe, MT 59071
(406)328-6830   (406) 328-6857 fax
e-mail: jchilds@mcn.net

Season: May 15 to September 15   Guest capacity: 15   Airport: Billings, MT

Genuine Ranch Vacation Is Ideal For Families.
Our ranch is 4th generation, family owned and operated, we take one family or party at a time. Come sleep in an historic log lodge built in 1907. Eat in the CookHouse with crew and the owners. Help move and doctor cattle, build fence, clean ditches, or hike, swim, fish and hunt on 15,000 acres in the foothills of the Beartooth Mountains just over the mountains from Yellowstone National Park.

Travel tip: Don't take your expensive show saddles on vacation where they may be rained on. Take your old trail saddle. When you are at a guest ranch riding the ranches horses use their well broken in saddles for a comfortable ride.

MONTANA
Seven Lazy P
Guest Ranch 🤠🐴
P.O. Box 178
Choteau, MT 59422
(406)466-2044

Season: May 1-November 30
Guest capacity: 20
Airport: Great Falls, MT

Quiet Solitude and Scenic Beauty.
Chuck and Sharon Blixrud invite you to visit
them and share in their ranch set deep in the
Teton River Canyon. Native log cabins and lodge house house guests. Corrals of good mountain
horses await to show you the high country, wild rivers, and abundant wildlife. Mule and white tail
deer, Rocky Mountain goats, big horn sheep, moose, black bear and perhaps a rare silvertip grizzly
may be found. Wonderful fly fishing, excellent photography, thousands of wildflowers. Ranch stays
or pack into the Bob Marshall Wilderness.

MONTANA
Sixty Three Ranch 🤠🐴
P.O. Box 979
Livingston, MT 59047
(406)222-0570   (406)222-9446 fax
Web: www.ranchweb.com/63ranch

Season: Mid-June to Mid-September
Guest capacity: 30
Airport: Bozeman, MT, pickup available

Vacation at a National Historic Site, Dating From 1863.
At 63 horses out number guests more than two to one. You'll admire the condition and quality of our
stock. Morning and afternoon rides daily, all-day rides, over 100 miles of trails. Walk-trot-lope rides.
Guests often join the cowboys in moving cattle and learning to lasso. Pack trips into the Absaroka/
Beartooth Wilderness north of Yellowstone Park. Tucked among the aspen, log and frame cabins with
private baths, welcome singles, couples or families with comfort, peace and privacy. Our meals get
raves from our guests. World famous fishing in Blue Ribbon creeks and rivers. Video available.

NEW HAMPSHIRE
Chebacco Dude Ranch 🤠🐴
Rt 153
S. Effingham, NH 03882
(603)522-3211

Season: March-December   Guest capacity: 10-15   Airport: Rochester, NH

Best Little Dude Ranch in New Hampshire...Great for the Whole Family!
If it's riding our hundred miles of trails...dining on home cooked meals...relaxing in our jacuzzi...or
resting in our quiet rooms... a Chebacco Dude Ranch vacation will satisfy all you "City Slickers". Full
package vacation includes three meals daily and unlimited riding through picturesque forest, and
scenic mountain or lakeside trails. Free riding lessons. Activities - canoeing, swimming, golfing or
movie, pool or western dancing in our entertainment center.

NEW YORK
Pinegrove Dude Ranch 🍴🐴

P.O. Box 209, 30 Cherrytown Road
Kerhonkson, NY 12446
(800)926-9825   (914)626-7345   (914)626-7365 fax
e-mail: pinegrove@ulster.net   Web: www.pinegroveranch.com
Season: Year-round   Guest capacity: 400   Airports: Newburgh, JFK & LaGuardia or Newark, NJ

**ABC & CNN News Rate Pinegrove a "Super Adventure", Fox 5 "Thrilling Vacation ".
Designated 1992 Family Resort of the Year by Family Circle Magazine.**
Rustic informal, family oriented dude ranch. Free snack bar, included: thirty indoor/outdoor sports facilities, boating and fishing, horseback riding, cattle drives. Walk-trot-canter rides. Fully supervised children's day camp, nursery and night patrol Three hardy meals daily, entertainment and hayrides. Two ski slopes with free rentals and snow making on premises. WE LOVE KIDS!

NEW YORK
Ridin-Hy Ranch 🍴

Sherman Lake
Warrensburg, NY 12885
(518)494-2742

Season: Year-round
Guest capacity: 200
Airport: Albany, NY

**800 Acres on Sherman Lake
in the 6 Million Acre
Adirondack StatePark.**
Horseback riding through beautiful
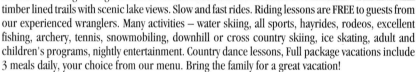
timber lined trails with scenic lake views. Slow and fast rides. Riding lessons are FREE to guests from our experienced wranglers. Many activities – water skiing, all sports, hayrides, rodeos, excellent fishing, archery, tennis, snowmobiling, downhill or cross country skiing, ice skating, adult and children's programs, nightly entertainment. Country dance lessons, Full package vacations include 3 meals daily, your choice from our menu. Bring the family for a great vacation!

NEW YORK
Rocking Horse Ranch Resort 🍴

600 Rte 44 - 55
Highland, NY 12528
(800)647-2624 or (914)691-2927 (914)691-6434 fax
e-mail: buckyrhr@aol.com Web: www.rhranch.com
Season: Year-round   Guest capacity: 400
Airports: Newark, NJ; Newburgh, JFK and LaGuardia, NY

"New York's Premier Ranch Resort".
For three years Family Circle Magazine's readers poll have given us the "Favorite Family Resort" Award. Ride over 500 acres of mountain and orchard trails surrounding our lake. The whole family can find an activity at a price you can afford, water skiing, paddle boats, fishing, dancing, tennis, indoor & outdoor pools, hay & buggy rides, ball games, miniature golf, indoor rifle & archery. Enjoy comfortable accommodations and all-you-can-eat-choice-menus. Same family hosts since 1958. Join us this year. AAA-3 Diamond Rating. Walk-trot-canter riding.

NEW YORK
Roseland Ranch Resort ⌖
Stanfordville, NY 12581
(800)431-8292
Season: Year-round
Guest capacity: 300
Airports: Newark, NJ, JFK and LaGuardia, NY

**East Meets West at New York's
Favorite Family Ranch Resort.**

The Wheel of Fortune, Jeopardy and the Price is Right give their contestants fantastic vacations at Roseland Ranch resort in Dutchess county. Roseland Ranch is nestled on 1,000 acres of rolling hills with groomed trails. Roseland Ranch is a "Family Affair", catering to city slickers young and old. Free activities include unlimited horseback riding, early morning breakfast rides, evening rides, tennis, indoor and outdoor pools, indoor riding arena, ball games, 3 full meals daily, snowmobiling, skiing, rifle range and electronic arcade.

OHIO
Heartland Country Resort ⌖⌖🐎
2994 Township Road 190
Fredericktown, OH 43019
(800)230-7030 or (419)768-9300
Web: www.bbhost.com/heartland
Season: Year-round   Guest capacity: 40   Airport: Columbus, OH

Rated "Excellent" by the American Bed & Breakfast Association.
And a riding stable with many registered horses. Recreation and relaxation abound, with riding in arenas or on wooded trails, swim in the heated pool, play pool in the recreation room or cross-country ski over the rolling countryside, compete in a game of basketball, ping pong, or horseshoes, lounge on the deck or screened porch, have a candle lit meal in the 1878 dining room, watch movies in the sitting room, AND unwind in your private Jacuzzi at day's end. Near state forest trail systems.

OREGON
Rock Springs Guest Ranch
64201 Tyler Road ⌖🍷
Bend, OR 97701
(800)225-3833   (541)382-1957
(541)382-7774 fax
e-mail: info@rocksprings.com
Web: www.rocksprings.com

Season: June 19-August 31 guest ranch;
Sept.-June Conference Center for groups
Guest capacity: 50   Airport: Redmond, OR

Nestled in the foothills of the Cascade Mountain Range.
Rock Springs accommodates only 50 guests, the atmosphere is warm and homey, and the service is always personal. Our Summer American Plan runs from the end of June through August. The week long program includes three delicious meals each day, comfortable lodging in our cozy cabins, a fantastic youth program for children ages 3 to 5 and 6 to 12, and great outdoor activities, horseback riding, swimming, tennis, volleyball, hayrides. Sept.-June conference center, offering exclusive use to groups of 20 or more.

PENNSYLVANIA
Buck Valley Ranch 🐎
Rt 2, Box 1170
Warfordsburg, PA 17267-9667
(800)294-3759   (717) 294-3759
e-mail: buckvalleyranch@worldnet.att.net   Web: www.pafarmstay.com/buckvalleyranch
Season: Year-round   Guest capacity: 8   Airport: Hagerstown, MD

Enjoy Our Peaceful Valley and Relaxing Atmosphere from Horseback.
We are centrally located just 2 hours from Baltimore, Washington D.C. and Pittsburgh in the scenic Appalachian Mountains of southern Pennsylvania. Riding is our main attraction. Enjoy horseback riding through 2,000 acres of woodlands. All meals are delicious, healthy and filling. Comfortable accommodations are in a 4 bedroom farmhouse. Pool and sauna located on premises. Nearby attractions include canoeing, skiing, fishing and golf. Family packages available during the week.

PENNSYLVANIA
Flying W Ranch 🐎 🐎
Star Route 2, Box 150
Tionesta, PA 16353
(814)463-7663
Season: April to Mid-December
Guest capacity: 100 Airport: Pittsburgh, PA

A Dude Ranch for Horse People .
Enjoy our scenic cabins and long rides through the Allegheny Mountains. Ride our horses or bring your own, stabling available. Park your camper in our campgrounds or forest wilderness camps. Join our yearly Organized Trail Rides. Enjoy the Allegheny Mountain Championship Rodeo or American Indian Pow-Wow. Schedule a mountain pack trip. Send your child to our Summer Camp. Something for all riders and non-rider companions.

SOUTH DAKOTA

Triple "R" Ranch

P.O. Box 124
Keystone, SD 57751-0124
(888)RRR-ANCH or (605)666-4605

Season: Year-round
Guest capacity: 15   Airport: Rapid City, SD

Family Fun in A Leisurely Western Atmosphere.
Venture off the beaten path and experience--daily horseback riding into the devastatingly beautiful Norbeck & Black Elk Wilderness; the world famous mountain carvings--Mount Rushmore and Crazy Horse memorials; chuckwagon supper, western history, cowboy poetry, fresh air, stars galore, tasty home cooking, relaxation, & personal attention all wrapped into one terrific package--topped off with our own Triple "R" brand of western hospitality!

TEXAS

Bald Eagle Ranch

P.O. Box 1177
Bandera, TX 78003-1177
(830)460-3012 or Fax: (830)460-3013
E-mail: info@baldeagle
Web: www.baldeagleranch.com

Season: Year-round
Guest capacity: 16
Airport: San Antonio, TX, pickup available

Are You Looking for a
Rewarding Western Ranch Experience?
Bald Eagle Ranch is Your Choice!
Our emphasis is on horseback riding, covering 6,000 acres. All our horses are registered Quarter horses from the age of 5, geared to your individual riding ability. Enjoy our fine herd of Texas Longhorns. Relax in the Jacuzzi or take a swim in our pool. Do some skeet shooting or archery. Our culinary trained chef makes sure that eating time is one of the daily events. First class accommodations in all suite cabins. Excellent conference service for up to 16 participants. (No children under 16)

TEXAS

Green Acres Ranch
and Equestrian Club

576 Sabine Creek Rd.
Royse City, TX 75189
(972)636-2007
e-mail: garec@onramp.net
Web: www.greenacresranch.com

Season: Year-round   Guest capacity: 20+Airport: Dallas, TX

One of the Nicest Dude Ranches in Texas.
2,000 acres of trails, creeks, rivers, lakes and woods. Well trained horses for every ability. We have 12 gaited horses, Tennessee Walkers, Missouri Fox Trotters and Rackers for a smooth ride. Ride all day and enjoy our swimming pool and hot tub, tennis court, ponds for fishing, and meeting rooms for groups. Marvelous meals. In the area find several golf courses, 2 large lakes for water skiing and boat rides, plus the night spots of Dallas just a short drive away.

TEXAS
Running R Ranch 🐎
Rt 1, Box 590, RR 1077
Bandera, TX 78003
(830)796-3984
e-mail: runningr@texas.net
Web: www.rrranch.com
Season: Year-round Guest capacity: 45
Airport: San Antonio, TX

Live The "Real West", In Bandera,
The Cowboy Capital Of The World.

Running R Ranch is a guest ranch with it's focus on horseback riding. Ride through the unspoiled beauty of our ranch and the 5,500 acre Hill Country State Natural Area where we do most of our riding. Learn from experienced wranglers about ranching, cattle, horses, or take lessons in our arena. Enjoy a stay on a ranch where you arrive as a guest and leave as a friend.

TEXAS
Twin Elm Ranch 🐎
P.O. Box 117
Bandera, TX 78003
(830)796-3628 phone / fax
Season: Year-round   Guest capacity: 70   Airport: San Antonio, TX

Twin Elm Ranch Is A Genuinely Western Guest Ranch.

The romantic, picturesque, Texas Hill Country, overlooking the Medina River. The perfect place to relax, forget your cares and enjoy the happy-go-lucky life of the Old West. We offer horseback riding, clean, comfortable, air-conditioned lodging, all the ranch style food you can eat, campfires and hayrides, amateur rodeo, and swimming in our pool. Ride the rapids on crystal clear Medina River. Friday and Saturday nights, enjoy dances with live western music in famous Bandera nightspots.

Green Acres Ranch and Equestrian Club

5736 Sabine Creek Rd.
Royce City, TX 75189
972-636-2007
www.greenacresranch.com
e-mail: garec@onramp.net

One of the nicest Dude Ranches in Texas. Visit us while you are in the Dallas area. Lodging for over 20 people with great food and hospitality. Amenities include: swimming pool and hot tub, tennis court, fishing ponds, stables and pens, large arena, round pen, over 6 hours of trails on two thousand acres, creeks and rivers, woods, and large open pastures (see cattle grazing). We also take visitors to a West Texas Ranch (along the Brazos River) and to Oklahoma trails. Our ranch is located between two large lakes where we water ski and boat ride in good weather. We have gaited horses, Tennessee Walkers, Missouri Fox Trotters and Rackers. All horses are safe, calm and comfortable with good dispositions. Horses for any riding ability. There is a 5,000 sq. foot room for meetings, dancing, or large dinners or meetings. Several golf courses and night spots are within 10 to 15 minutes away.

Come for a relaxing vacation or schedule your meeting here.

WISCONSIN
Woodside Ranch ![western riding icon]

W 4015 State Hwy 82
Mauston, WI 53948
1-800-626-4275 or (608) 847-4275
Season: Year-round   Guest capacity: 150   Airport: Madison, WI

Winner Family Circle Award for Being Among the 5 Best Ranch Resorts in the Country.
Woodside also has achieved a 2★ listing in the Mobile Travel Guide for Ranch Resorts. Family owned and operated, 1,000 acre working ranch in South/Central Wisconsin. Fireplace log cabins. Full service American Plan, all activities included, horseback riding, covered wagon rides, pony ring, tennis, mini-golf, hay rides, breakfast rides, Buffalo cookouts, barn dances, pool, skiing, and winter sleigh rides.

WYOMING
Absaroka Mountain Lodge ![western riding icon] ![take your own horse icon]

1231 E. Yellowstone Hwy
Wapiti, WY 82450
(307) 587-3963
e-mail: bkudelski@wyoming.com
Season: May 1-September 25   Guest capacity: 50   Airport: Cody, WY

Visit Yellowstone, the Nations Oldest National Park.
Our scenic mountain Guest Ranch is located just outside the Park! Come stay in our comfortable cabins, our program includes breakfast and dinner, and many activities such as fishing, hiking, touring, hunting and guided mountain horseback rides into the backcountry. Miles of trails to ride through the Shoshone National Forest and two wilderness areas. Bring your own horses if you wish, we have corrals at the ranch to accommodate them. Call us for more information.

WYOMING
Boulder Lake Lodge ![western riding icon]

P.O. Box 1100 - HL
Pinedale, WY 82941
(800)788-5401 or (307)537-5400

Season: Mid-June-Mid-September
Guest capacity: 20
Airport: Jackson Hole, WY

**Wind River Mountains –
Remote and Rugged.**
Enjoy the heart of the Rocky Mountains from our comfortable, yet rustic lodge. Surrounded by National Forest, the lodge is truly "at the end of the road". Trail riding for all levels of skill, from children's rides to extended high mountain pack trips. Cookouts, breakfast/dinner rides, "Mule drawn" hayrides, boating, swimming, excellent fishing and hiking also available. Full "ranch style" meals prepared from scratch. Wonderful variety, fresh vegetables and fruits, tender meats, homemade pastry, served buffet style. Wilderness pack trips into the Wind River Range.

![western saddle icon] Western Riding   ![english saddle icon] English Riding   ![horse in trailer icon] Take Your Own Horse   ![cowboy hat icon] Dude Ranch Association Members

WYOMING
CM Ranch 🐎

P.O. Box 217
Dubois, WY 82513
(307) 455-2331   (307) 455-3984 fax
e-mail: cmranch@wyoming.com

Season: June to September   Guest capacity: 55
Airport: Jackson Hole, WY, pickup available

**The CM Ranch is One of the Most Beautiful,
Really Old-Time Historic Ranches in Wyoming**
You can ride, fish, hike, swim in the outdoor pool, picnic, or relax with a book. Horses are matched to your ability and rides go out twice a day except Sundays. The ranch is contiguous to the Fitzpatrick Wilderness and Shoshone National Forest, which allows for almost endless private riding country of great variety and beauty. The ranch's home water, Jakey's Fork, or nearby Wind River, offer exceptional fly-fishing. A variety of evening activities and entertainment are enjoyed by all ages.

WYOMING
Flying A Ranch 🐎

Rt 1, Box 7
Pinedale, WY 82941
(800)678-6543 winter
(307)367-2385 summer
e-mail: flyinga@wyoming.com
Web: www.flyinga.com

Season: June 15-October 1   Guest capacity: 12   Airport: Jackson Hole, WY

The Rustic Elegance of Our Cabins and Cuisine Assure You a Fresh Perspective.
The historic Flying A Ranch, located 50 miles southeast of Jackson Hole, offers distinctive western vacations for discerning adults. Come stay in luxurious cabins, enjoy delicious cuisine and relax. Every day can be filled with excitement or relaxation. Experience horseback riding in the high country, observing and photographing wildlife, trout fishing and hiking in the Majestic Northern Rockies. Yellowstone and Grand Teton National Parks are only a short drive away.

WYOMING
Lozier's Box "R" Ranch

Box 100 - HLVG
Cora, WY 82925
(800)822-8466 or (307)367-4868
e-mail: info@boxr.com
Web: www.boxr.com

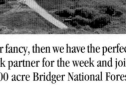

Season: June - Sept.
Guest capacity: 25
Airport: Jackson Hole, WY

Ranch Based Horseback Vacations for Adults, Singles and Families.
If a working ranch vacation is your life long dream; and cowboys, good horses and gettin' up at dawn strikes your fancy, then we have the perfect get-away for you! Team up with your own personal four legged work partner for the week and join us movin' cattle, wranglin' the cavvy, riding for hours in the 840,000 acre Bridger National Forest and so much more. All-inclusive stays.

WYOMING
The Hideout
at Flitner Ranch

3208 Beaver Creek Road
Greybull, WY 82426
1-800-FLITNER (354-8637)
Web: www.thehideout.com

Season: June - September
Airport: Cody, WY

Ranch Resort, Cowboy Adventures.
A working cattle ranch, founded in 1906, is located in the beautiful rolling foothills of the majestic Big Horn Mountains of Wyoming. Today it offers the opportunity for guests to experience the traditional ranch life as well as other outdoor activities while enjoying upscale rustic western accommodations. Video available. See our ad on the inside front cover.

WYOMING
Ranger Creek
Guest Ranch

P.O. Box 47
Shell, WY 82441
(888) 817-SPUR or (614) 431-9265
e-mail: billc@netset.com
Web: www.netset.com/~billc

Season: Year-round   Guest capacity: 25
Airport: Sheridan, WY or Billings, MT

Where the Spirit of the Old West Remains.
Established in 1919, Ranger Creek Guest Ranch sits in a high mountain meadow atop the Bighorn National Forest. This picturesque setting offers a variety of western style riding ranging from 1 hour to all day trips. Other activities include wagon rides, black powder shooting, fishing, hiking, hunting, pack trips, photography, snowmobiling, cross-country skiing or just sit back and enjoy the abundant wildlife. Children will enjoy our Little Pardoner's Program. Relax in log cabins with private baths and dine in the main lodge overlooking a meadow of wildflowers.

NEW MEXICO

Rancho Cañón Ancho

Ride into the
Old Wild West on
Your Own Horse
or One of Ours!

P.O. Box 303 • Wagon Mound, NM 87752 • **(505) 666-2004**

WYOMING
Triangle C Ranch 🤠
3737 US Hwy 26
Dubois, WY 82513
(307) 455-2225   (307) 455-2031 fax
Season: June - October   Guest capacity: 50   Airport: Jackson, WY

Majestic Absaroka Mountains, Warm Hospitality, and Great Trail Riding.
Join the Garnick family for a week you will always treasure in your memories. For over 50 years they have been entertaining families. You'll enjoy your own private log cabin, nestled in a forested area surrounded by the Shoshone National Forest. Each guest has their own horse for the week to enjoy daily trail rides. Lots to do - evening programs, hot tub, river swimming, fishing, cookouts, square dancing, hiking, river floating, canoeing, gymkhana, rodeo...

WYOMING
Triple EEE Guest Ranch 🐎
Rt. 287
P.O. Box 538
Dubois, WY 82513
(800) 353-2555 or (307) 455-2304
e-mail: tripllee@aol.com
Web: www.dudesville.com
Season: June - September
Guest capacity: 10
Airports: Jackson, or Riverton WY

Western Fun for the Entire Family.
Located 80 miles from Yellowstone, this high mountain guest ranch offers the same majestic scenery as our nations most loved national park. Wait till you see the panoramic view right from our wraparound porch! Unlimited horseback riding takes you through the ruggedly beautiful Absaroka mountains. Help find and roundup cattle for shipment. Other activities include trout fishing, line dancing, western cookouts, sing alongs and much more. Cabins or lodge available.

ENGLISH STYLE RIDING ADVENTURES

Enjoy riding on an English saddle during your vacation. Find instruction or trail ride.

IRELAND
The Aille Cross
Equestrian Center 🐎

Rt. 2 Box 331B
Charleston, WV 25314
(800)757-1667 Fax: (304)744-2324
Season: Oct.-April;
        fox hunting, Mid-Oct. - end of Feb.
Airport: Shannon, Ireland

The Aille Cross-Country Trail
Offers a Wide Variety of Options.
From trail riding and jumping over natural
cross-country obstacles to schooling over
our professionally designed cross-country course at Dartfield, to foxhunting with the Galway Blazers.
We are able to accommodate all levels of riders, from beginning jumpers to those with years of
experience. Ireland's mile climate provides wonderful weather for riding year round.

MAINE
Speckled Mountain Ranch 🐎

RR 2, Box 717
Bethel, ME 04217
(207) 836-2908
Season: May - October   Guest capacity: 4 riders, 8 guests   Airport: Portland, ME

Our Intention is to Create a Challenging and Rewarding Riding Experience
Explore miles of beautiful mountain scenery on horses who enjoy their jobs. 2-5 day trail riding
packages for experienced riders who can handle a horse at all gaits over varied terrain. Advanced
riders will enjoy galloping up the Miles Notch Trail, crossing the Pleasant River, jumping a log or two
along the way. Instruction for less experienced riders, learn more about riding and horse care.

VERMONT
Mountain Top Inn
and Resort 🐎🐎

Mountain Top Road
Chittenden, VT 05737
Reservations for Riding Vacations 1-800-648-TROT (8768)

Season: May to October   Guest capacity: 150   Airport: Burlington, or Rutland, VT

Elegant Four-Season Country Inn Resort.
The home of Vermont Riding Vacations. Spectacular views, relaxing atmosphere and fine dining.
Trail ride up to 6 hours per day, or take English or Western lessons in equitation, jumping, dressage
or introduction to cross-country. In addition, enjoy swimming, canoeing, kayaking, fly-fishing, golf
& golf school, tennis, claybird shooting, mountain biking and hiking. Cross-country skiing and sleigh
rides in winter. A wonderful destination for equestrians with non-rider companions, there are many
activities for all.

VIRGINIA
The Conyers House Inn
& Stable

3131 Slate Mills Road
Sperryville, VA 22740
(540) 987-8025
e-mail: conyers@msninc.com
Web: www.bnb-n-va.com/conyers.htm

Season: Year-round   Guest capacity: 16   Airport: Charlottesville or Dulles

Marvelous Inn, Offering Fox Hunting, Cross Country Jumping or Trail Rides.
Located in the midst of Virginia's most beautiful Hunt Country, in the Blue Ridge foothills. Fox hunting and hill topping are available for experienced riders. We have spectacular cross country trails for the novice or expert rider. An excellent opportunity to get legged up. Eight rooms with private bathrooms, fireplaces, and A/C. Ten porches. Delicious breakfasts and dinner here.

VIRGINIA
The Equestrian Centre
at Penmeryl Farm

P.O. Box 402
Greenville, VA 24440
(800) 808-6617 or (540) 337-0622

Season: Year-round   Guest capacity: 45   Airport: Charlottesville, VA

A First-Class Equestrian Resort, Located on 375 Acres in the Scenic Shenandoah Valley.
We offer Equestrian training and comfortable accommodations in an elegant country setting. Riding programs are tailored for each individual guest, all levels can benefit. Experienced instructors cover all English riding disciplines, from Hunter/Jumper to Dressage, and Eventing. Includes a 32 acre cross-country course. Accommodations in our lodge or our new cabins. Also a wide variety of resort activities, two lakes for fishing, and sailing with a wonderful beach, tennis, swimming pool and jacuzzi.

VIRGINIA
The Hunting Box

Rt. 620
P.O. Box 226
Boyce, VA 22620
(540)837-2160   (540)837-2110 fax

Seasons: Hunting – October thru March
           Lessons & Workshops – April thru August
Guest capacity: 12 people, 10 horses

Accommodations for Horses & Riders in the "Hunt Country of America".
For experienced riders, hunting is available with most hunts in northern Virginia. A limited number of Hirelings are available. Riding lessons & Horsemanship Workshops are offered, Spring & Summer. Facilities include indoor ring and swimming pool.

When contacting these fine destinations, please tell them
you found them through the Horse Lovers Vacation Guide.

EXPERIENCED RIDER ADVENTURES

Join us for a true challenging adventure put together to suit experienced riders.
All participants **must be** proficient at controlling their horses at all gaits.

ARIZONA
The Horseshoe Ranch on Bloody Basin Road
HCR 34, Box 5005
Mayer, AZ 86333
(520)632-8813   e-mail: hranch@primenet.com
Season: September - June   Guest capacity: 12   Airport: Phoenix, AZ

Experienced Riders, Become Part of the Team That Rides For the Horseshoe Brand.
Experienced riders come to do what they have never done before – work cattle from the saddle of
a cattle-savvy ranch horse. Riders find doing real cowboy work the "Ultimate High". 70,000 acres of
mesas, canyons and mountains in snow-free Arizona. Saddle up and do what needs to be done that
day, sorting, searching for strays, gathering, driving, roping, riding fence, branding and doctoring.
Then shower off the trail dust in your own private ranch house room and enjoy a hearty ranch meal.

COLORADO
Lost Valley Ranch
29555 Goose Creek Road, Box HL
Sedalia, CO 80135
(303)647-2311   (303)647-2315 fax
e-mail: lostranch@aol.com
Web: www.ranchweb.com/lost

Season: March 1-December 1
Guest capacity: 95
Airport: Denver or Colorado Springs, CO

**Discover Our Year-'round Authentic
Working Cattle/Horse Ranch.**
Just 80 miles from Denver or Colorado Springs. Blaze new trails while exploring 26,000 acres of the
Rocky Mountains. We have year 'round riding, cattle roundups, special horsemanship weeks, weekly
rodeos and an Orvis fly-fishing school. AAA rated "4 Diamonds." Cabin suites with fireplace. Weekly
all-inclusive adult rates per person: $1,695(summer); $700-$1,290,(fall-spring).

TENNESSEE
Flintlock Farm
790 G'Fellers Road
Chuckey, TN 37641
(423)257-2489   (423) 257-5547 fax   e-mail: flintloc@aol.com
Season: Year-round   Guest capacity: 6   Airport: Tri-Cities, pickup available

Challenging Riding Adventures in the Land of the First Pioneers.
Come ride with us on beautiful Blue Ridge mountain and valley trails. Create your own package
combining unlimited riding with fishing, rafting, canoeing, hiking, and hot-air ballooning. Spectacular mountain views from our lovingly restored and furnished 200 year old log farmhouse. We
welcome small groups of experienced riders with warm Southern hospitality, personal attention,
cozy accommodations, and great country cooking!

HORSE FARMS & RANCHES

Enjoy the country on a farm or ranch that raises horses.

SOUTH DAKOTA
Dakota Badland Outfitters
P.O. Box 85
Custer, SD 57730
(605)673-5363
Web: www.wordpros.com/dakota

Season: May 15 to October 8   Guest capacity: 2 - 10
Airport: Rapid City Regional Airport

Ride the Remote Badlands National Park or the Black Hills National Forest.
This authentic working horse ranch offers horseback expeditions into the remote Badlands National Park, and the Black Hills National Forest, ride trails or choose a working ranch visit allowing guests a "hands on" experience. Take part in the day to day activities of a **real working horse ranch**. Guests can customize their visit by emphasizing **starting colts**, introduction to **roping**, or **western horsemanship cowboy style.**

TEXAS
Knolle Farm & Ranch
Barn, Bed & Breakfast
Rt. 1, Box 81, Farm Road 70
Sandia, TX 78383
(512) 547-2546   (512) 547-3934 fax
Web: www.knolle.com
Season: Year-round   Guest capacity: 18   Airport: Corpus Christi, TX

Bed, Barn and Breakfast in a Renovated Historic 1939 Dairy Barn.
Knolle Jersey Farms boasted the "World's Largest Jersey Herd" for over 60 years, now it pampers guests. Nestled in the Nueces River Valley, amid towering oaks and lush, rolling fields. Western & English riding, cattle roundups and acres of trails. Guests with private horses find spacious barns, paddocks, and 2 riding arenas. Upscale guest cottages are filled with antiques, & full kitchens. Fishing, canoeing, game room, golf carts, and guided hunting on premises. Catered gourmet meals. Birdwatching, on the Great Texas Coastal Birding Trail. Fun for all wanting individual attention.

VERMONT
Vermont Icelandic Horse Farm
P.O. Box 577
Waitsfield, VT 05673
(802)496-7141   (802)496-5390 fax
Season: Year-round   Airport: Burlington, VT

Experience the Exceptional Riding Comfort and Stamina of the Icelandic Horse.
Vermont Icelandic Horse Farm offers scenic trail rides year-round on one of the most comfortable riding horses in the world. Summer or winter riding is truly an unforgettable experience on our gaited horses from Iceland. We offer trail rides of varying lengths, and unique Inn to Inn packages, including all meals, and lodging. Come and visit our farm and get to know the very special Icelandic Horse. Sale horses are also available. For more information and a color brochure, please call 802-496-7141.

HORSE TREKKING

Ride each day on a prescribed route stopping each night at a B&B or quaint country inn.

CALIFORNIA
Ricochet Ridge Ranch 🐴🐴
24201 N Hwy 1
Fort Bragg, CA 95437
(707) 964-7669
Season: Year-round Airport: San Francisco
or Ukiah Municipal, CA

Gallop Along Scenic Costal Beaches.
Horse Trekking adventures, riding along
Northern California's wild Mendocino
beaches, through majestic redwood forests.
Nightly accommodations at B&B Inns, with
hot tubs. Fully catered, including fine California wines and nightly entertainment. Also endurance
riding seminars. English or western, dressage and endurance winning horses. You won't believe the
quality of the horses! Bring your own if you wish. Novice to advanced riders welcome. Instruction
available.

CANADA – Québec
Au Jal A Cheval, Inc. 🐴
82, Rang XII
Auclair, Québec, Canada G0L 1A0
(418)899-6635

Season: May 15 - October 15   Airport: Mont-Joli, Québec   Guest capacity: 10

The Most Beautiful Vacation on Horseback.
Discover the grandeur of our 150 miles of trails through the lakes, mountains and rivers of the
Northern Appalachians in Québec, Canada. Enjoy a different cottage every night and hearty meals
served by our attentive staff. A thrilling ride in the heart of nature for everyone who loves horses and
freedom. Wonderful vacations for horse lovers.

FLORIDA
Back In The Saddle...🐴
In Florida!
P.O. Box 60079
Fort Myers, FL 33906-6079
(941)368-0760 or (800)296-0249

Season: April, October and November   Airport: Fort Meyers, FL   Guest Capacity: 14

Ride From the Atlantic Ocean to the Gulf of Mexico Beaches.
In between, ride ranches and dairies, orange groves and sugar cane fields, lakes and rivers, a
Seminole Indian Reservation, and the Everglades. Subtropical wildlife, wildflowers and visits with
locals make this a study of the "real" Florida that had cattle and cowmen before Texas. Nationally-
known staff. High support level. All riding levels. Many riders return yearly.

IRELAND
The Connemara Trail 🐎
Aile Cross Equestrian Center
County Galway, IRELAND
U.S. representative: Laura Pray
Crazy Oaks Farm
Rt 2, Box 331B
Charleston, WV 25314
(800)757-1667
(304)744-2324 fax

Season: End of April-September
Airport: Shannon, Ireland

The Connemara Trail Rides Offer Western or English Riding...
across the mountains and beaches of the west coast of Ireland. This is not just a vacation for experienced riders but for anyone who would enjoy seeing the dramatic Irish countryside from the back of a horse. Our rides are six day adventures in Connemara, one of the most rugged and beautiful parts of Ireland. We travel from point to point each day, often through areas inaccessible by car or bike. Guests choose either first class Irish country hotels or B&B's.

MEXICO
Saddling South
Baja Pack Trips 🐎
P.O. Box 827
Calistoga, CA 94515
1-800-398-6200
(707) 942-4550 phone/fax

e-mail: tourbaja@iname.com
web: www.tourbaja.com

Season: October-May   Guest capacity: 3-8
Airport: Loreto, or Baja California Sur,
        Mexico. Airport pickup available.

Grab Your Sombrero for an Incredible Journey, into the Heart of the Sierra Giganta.
Saddling South takes you along volcanic ridges, through cactus garden valleys and into the lush palm springs in Baja's spectacular desert mountains. Owner Trudi Angell, with 20 years experience exploring this magnificent peninsula, offers a chance to learn traditions and histories of the remote ranching lifestyle unique to Baja, Mexico. Join us as our local guides share their wisdom and lore along the original missionary trails of the Californias.

MONTANA

Montana
Equestrian Tours ⲧ ⲟ

P.O. Box 1280
Swan Valley, MT 59826
(406)754-2900 or
(800)484-5757 Ext. 0096
e-mail: cnd2900@montana.com
Web: www.seeleyswanpathfinder.com/pfbusiness/mtequestriantours/horse.html

Season: June to September   Guest capacity: 10   Airport: Missoula, MT

Climb Aboard the Swan Valley Wilderness Ride...
Experience the spectacular sights of the secluded, hidden gem of northwestern Montana's Swan Valley wilderness. Daily treks aboard fine mounts, 17 to 25 miles a day, deliver you nightly to sumptuous dining and accommodations at the valleys finest lodges. Trips run weekly, Sunday to Friday. Customized excursions available from any of our cooperating lodges with advance notice. Contact us for a brochure. Find out what our guests are saying about this remarkable adventure.

VERMONT

Kedron Valley Stables ⲟ

Route 106, P.O. Box 368
South Woodstock, VT 05071
Outside Vermont: (800)225-6301
In Vermont (802)457-1480 or
　　　(802)457-2734

Season: May-November
Guest capacity: 10
Airport Lebanon, NH

**Ride Between Picturesque
New England Country Inns.**

Kedron Valley has a variety of delightful vacation packages which allow you to ride across some of Vermont's most elegant carriage trails, through tranquil farmlands and wooded mountain trails. Enjoy lodging at Kedron Valley Inn or a variety of Country Inns located in Vermont's most beautiful historic towns. All-inclusive rates. Trail riding, Inn to Inn, mid-week trail riding clinics also.

WEST VIRGINIA

Swift Level ⲧ ⲟ 🐴

Rt 2, Box 269
Lewisburg, WV 24901
(304)645-1155

Season: April to November
Guest capacity: 12   Airport: Greenbrier Valley Airport

Ride the Appalachians.
Enjoy riding through the heartland of one of Americas's best kept secrets, in the Appalachian Mountains of West Virginia, on our world famous horses and Connemara ponies. Experience breathtaking views from high elevations. Pure mountain streams flanked by natural Rhododendron and lush farms in fertile valleys with pastures filled with cattle and sheep. Make this your opportunity to visit our part of the world. A place where Appalachian hospitality and culture await you.

HUNTING & FISHING GUIDES

COLORADO
Buffalo Horn Ranch 🐴
13825 County Rd. 7
Meeker, CO 81641
(970)878-5450   (970)878-4088 fax
Web: www.buffalohorn.com

Season: May-November
Guest Capacity: 30
Airport: Grand Junction, CO, pickup avail.

**Over 20,000+ Private Acres of
Breathtaking Scenery for Your
Hunting Adventure.**

You'll make it an annual event. Fully guided big game and bird hunts are available and come complete with lodging (in our beautiful new lodge), license, transportation, and game retrieval. We also have drop-camps with all the necessities. Supply your own food, sleeping bag and good hunting knowledge. Bird hunters will appreciate wingshooting at its finest for pheasant, quail, chukkar, and Hungarian partridge. If fishing is your sport, you'll enjoy our guided fly fishing trips on our private ponds or the famous White River. Please call or write for more information.

COLORADO
Wit's End Guest Ranch & Resort 🐴
254 Country Rd 500
Bayfield, CO 81122

(970) 884-4113

Season: Year-round   Airport: Durango, La Plata, CO   Guest Capacity: 66

For All Hunters and Fishermen.
Fishing available on the property in three large ponds, in the 6 mile long Lake Vallecito, rivers and 1/2 mile of semi-private stream fishing. Bait and fly-fishing with poles provided, instruction available. High country fishing throughout wilderness area. Day trips up to 4 miles along river, overnight and longer, 8 to 60 miles in the high country lakes and streams. Pack trips, overnight trips, through the Weminuche Wilderness with guides. Package and group rates. See also pack trips and color photos on pages 4 and 5.

MONTANA
Seven Lazy P Ranch 🐴
P.O. Box 178
Choteau, MT 59422   (406) 466-2044

Season: May to November   Airport: Great Falls, MT   Guest Capacity: 20

Explore the Bob Marshall Wilderness, Over a Million Acres to Fish or Hunt.
Well outfitted trips with one of Montana's top outfitters, through some of the most outstanding wilderness country in America. Ride the continental divide, view the Chinese Wall. Great mountain horses, comfortable camps, outstanding meals and a lot of time in the saddle. Recently voted Montana's #1 outfitter. Outstanding fishing, plentiful wildlife - Mule and Whitetail Deer, Rocky Mountain Goats, Bighorn sheep, Moose, Black Bear.

MONTANA
WTR Outfitters, Inc. ♞
520 Cooper Lake Rd
Ovando, MT 59854
1-800-WTR-5666 or
(406) 793-5666 phone/fax
e-mail: wtroutfitters@montana.com
Web: wtroutfitters.com

Season: June-December
Airport: Missoula, MT
Guest Capacity: 6 - 20

**Fishermen – Hunters: Have Your
Dream Trip Come True.**
Fully guided and outfitted trips. Summer roving fishing trips and fall hunting from horseback in the
Bob Marshall Wilderness complex. Fish for Rainbow, Brook, Eastern Brook and Bull Trout, Dolly
Varden and Grayling. Hunt Elk, Mule and Whitetail Deer, Black Bear, and by special permit Bighorn
Sheep, Moose and Rocky Mountain Goats.

WYOMING
Boulder
Lake Lodge ♞
P.O. Box 1100 - HL
Pinedale, WY 82941
1-800-788-5401 or (307) 537-5400

Season: September-October
Guest capacity: 6
Airport: Jackson Hole, WY

Ride the Winds!
Remote wilderness fishing and hunting trips.
Several species of trout in high lakes and
crystal clear streams with no competition from other fishermen. Excellent camp facilities and guides,
or spot pack trips for the self sufficient. Guided fall hunts for big elk, deer, moose and antelope.
Outstanding success in both fishing and hunting.

WYOMING / MONTANA
Sundance
Guest Ranch ♞
P.O. Box 458
Sundance, WY 82729
(800)521-4055
Season: Year-round   Guest Capacity: 32

So You Wanna Hunt and Fish.
You'll experience a special kind of hunt. When it comes to big game hunting the emphasis is on BIG.
Hunters may pursue the stately elk in his mountain retreat, track the mountain lion and black bear
or search the Aspen meadows for mule deer. Those who seek quiet leisure time can try their hand
at fishing our private stream, the clear water gurgling against the banks of the River.

LEARNING VACATIONS

Vacation while you learn more about riding and horses. Extend your knowledge of equitation, driving, roping, horse training, competition or horse packing techniques with varied possibilities through each destinations' special emphasis.

CALIFORNIA
Ricochet Ridge Ranch 🏇🐎
24201 N. Hwy 1
Fort Bragg, CA 95437
(707) 964-7669 phone/fax
Season: Year-round
Airport: San Francisco or Ukiah Municipal

Endurance Training Seminars.
Riding and sport horse conditioning instruction by Lari Shea, winner of the Tevis Cup 100 Mile Race. Beach and Redwood vacations on Northern California's Magnificent Mendocino Coast. Ride through majestic Redwood forests and along wild coastal beaches. Lodging, fine dining and entertainment at unique Bed & Breakfast Inns. Exceptional horses both English and Western.

COLORADO
Buffalo Horn Ranch 🏇
13825 County Rd. 7
Meeker, CO 81641
(970) 878-5450
Web: www.buffalohorn.com

Season: May - September   Airport: Grand Junction, CO   Guest Capacity: 30

Give Yourself a Royal Western Learning Adventure!
Professional instruction available for the novice or experienced rider, fisherman, or hunter. Test your skills at the best clay course in northwest Colorado. Fish our private ponds and the famous White River all within our 20,000+ acres of magnificent high country. Indulge in the creature comforts of gracious accommodations, a spacious lodge, and gourmet meals. Call or write for information.

EUROPE / ENGLAND / SCOTLAND / WALES
ITALY / FRANCE / SPAIN / COSTA RICA
Cross Country International Training Holidays Abroad 🐎

P.O. Box 1170
Millbrook, NY 12545
(800)828-TROT (8768)
Season, Airport and Guest Capacity vary

**Training Holidays with
Expert Instruction.**
Train in cross country jumping, show jumping, dressage and carriage driving. In England, Scotland, Wales, Ireland, Spain, and France.

Trail Riding Holidays.
Supervised and unsupervised trail rides in England, Scotland, Ireland, Wales, Italy, Spain, France and Costa Rica. Bed & Breakfast and Hotel accommodations available Inn to Inn or one location.

SOURI

S**ь**RT™ / Centered Riding®
Workshops for Adults
Brindabella Farms 🐎
5607 S. 222nd Road
Fair Grove, MO 65648
(417) 267-2900
Web: www.brindabellafarms.com
Season: March-December
Airport: Springfield, MO

Improve Your Riding Skills for Recreation or Competition.
Success-Centered Riding/Training (SCRT)
Workshops where dreams come true. Private or small groups. Experienced, caring Centered Riding instructors. Friendly school horses. Emphasizing confidence-building, physical conditioning, up-to-date information. Attractive facilities include lecture room, library, arenas, exercise room, sauna. English and Western riders welcomed. Enjoy the scenic Ozarks near Springfield. Brochure.

UTAH
All 'Round Ranch 🐎
P.O. Box 153 HL
Jensen, UT, 84035
(800) 603-8069 or (435) 789-7626
(435) 789-5902 fax
e-mail: allround@easilink.com
Web: www.allroundranch.com
Season: May - September   Guest Capacity: 12   Airport: Vernal, UT

Learn Cowboy Horsemanship on Quality Quarter Horses.
Four and six-day adventures scheduled summer through fall. Emphasis on active learning and full participation. Ride rugged rangeland in Utah and Colorado, camp at working cow camps, wrangle cattle. Horsemanship skills taught to all levels of riders, novice to experienced. Over 25 years in adventure-based education. Group size is limited; minimum age of 16, (12 on family adventures). Walk-trot-canter riding. Featured on the cover.

VERMONT
Kedron Valley Stables 🐎
Route 106, P.O. Box 368
South Woodstock, VT 05071
Outside Vermont (800) 225-6301
In Vermont (802) 457-1480

Season: May-November
Airport: Lebanon, NH   Guest Capacity: 10

Adult Trail Riding Clinics.
We have a variety of extremely talented instructors. Gain from hands-on experience in stable management, ground work, and some jumping, combined with trail riding, over many miles of scenic trails. Mid-week trail riding clinics, 5 nights 4 days, are a great introduction to mountain trail riding. Learn to traverse hilly terrain, cross streams and control your horse in open country. Includes lodging and gourmet meals.

VIRGINIA
The Conyers House Inn & Stable 🐴
3131 Slate Mills Road
Sperryville, VA 22740
(540) 987-8025
e-mail: conyers@msninc.com
Web: www.bnb-n-va.com/conyers.htm
Season: Year-round   Guest capacity: 16   Airport: Charlottesville or Dulles

Marvelous Inn, Offering Fox Hunting, Cross Country Jumping or Trail Rides.
Located in the midst of Virginia's most beautiful Hunt Country, the Blue Ridge foothills. Fox hunting and hill topping are available for experienced riders. We have spectacular cross country trails for the novice or expert. Excellent opportunity to get legged up. Eight rooms with private bathrooms, fireplaces, and A/C. Ten porches. Delicious breakfasts and dinner here.

VIRGINIA
The Hunting Box 🐴
Rt. 620
P.O. Box 226
Boyce, VA 22620
(540)837-2160   (540)837-2110 fax
Seasons: Fox Hunting – October thru March
        Lessons & Workshops – April thru August
Guest capacity: 12 people, 10 horses

Accommodations for Horses & Riders in the"Hunt Country of America".
For experienced riders, hunting is available with most hunts in northern Virginia. A limited number of Hirelings are available. Riding lessons & Horsemanship Workshops are offered, Spring & Summer. Facilities include indoor ring and swimming pool.

WYOMING
Yellowstone Institute 🐎
P.O. Box 117
Yellowstone National Park, WY 82190
(307)344-2294 (307)344-2485 fax
e-mail: dkline@yellowstoneassociation.org
Web: www.yellowstoneassociation.org

Season: June to September   Guest capacity: 8 to 14 per trip
Airport: Bozeman, MT Jackson Hole, WY

Educational Pack Trips Inside Yellowstone National Park.
The Yellowstone Institute is a non-profit field school operated in partnership with the National Park Service. We offer affordable 3-day, 4-day, and 5-day pack trips with emphasis on natural history, cultural history, and minimum impact camping. Join us for a unique educational experience in a spectacular wilderness setting. Please call or write for our free catalog.

When making inquiry, tell the destination site that you found them through the Horse Lovers Vacation Guide, for your best riding rates and schedules.

MUSEUMS, LIBRARIES & ATTRACTIONS

COLORADO
Arabian Horse Trust
12000 Zuni St.
Westminster, CO 80234-2300
(303)450-4710
You will find over 1,600 books, current and historical magazines, photographs, videos, films, farm & sale brochures, historical show programs and special collections.

COLORADO
ProRodeo Hall of Fame & Museum of the American Cowboy
101 Pro Rodeo Drive
Colorado Springs, CO 80919
(719)528-4764
Season: Year-round

The ONLY Museum in the World Devoted Exclusively to Rodeo - America's Original Sport.
Learn how rodeo evolved from it's origins in 19th century ranch work to becoming a major spectator sport, as documented in two multimedia presentations. In Heritage Hall you will view exhibits of historic and modern tools of the cowboy and rodeo trade - from saddles and ropes to clothing and hats. Rodeo greats, past and present, including current world champions, are honored in the Hall of Champions. See memorabilia, changing art exhibits and live rodeo animals, then you can visit the western and rodeo store. 1 Minute off I-25 in the heart of Pikes Peak Country.

IDAHO
Appaloosa Museum and Heritage Center
5070 Hwy. 8 W., P.O. Box 8403
Moscow, ID 83843-0903
(208)882-5578
Web:aphc@appaloosa.com
Artifacts related to the history of the Appaloosa, Native American horse tack, memorabilia, related to the development of the Appaloosa Horse Club. Information on annual trail rides.

FLORIDA
Austin Carriage Museum at Continental Acres
3000 Marion County Road
P.O. Box 68
Weirsdale, FL 32195
(352)750-5500   (352)753-3105 fax
e-mail: HorseResrt@aol.com
Web: www.continentalacres.com
Season: Year-round by appointment only

Historic Carriages.
A 36,000 square foot facility housing one of the largest private collections of historic horse drawn carriages in the United States. Over 70 carts, carriages, and coaches from around the world. Also related exhibits such as whips, harnesses, coaching horns, etc. help to round out the lively discussions on the "Carriage Era". Ninety minute guided tours. Group rates available.

FLORIDA
The Show Jumping Hall of Fame and Museum, Inc.
Information:
c/o Classic Communications
38 Mechanic St, Suite 101
Foxboro, MA 02035-2042
(508)698-6810
Located inside Busch Gardens, Tampa, FL
Season: Year-round
Admission: Must go through
                    Busch Gardens Park admission.
Of Interest To Jumpers.
Photos, exhibits from show jumping history plus plaques honoring the men, women and horses.

KENTUCKY
American Saddle Horse Museum
4093 Iron Works Pike
Lexington, KY 40511-8401
(606) 259-2746
e-mail: asbfan@aol.com
Web: www.american-saddlebred.com
Season: Year-round

Dedicated to the American Saddlebred.
A privately owned attraction located at the Kentucky Horse Park (I-75, Exit 120). Come discover the American Saddlebred Horse, Kentucky's native breed. Multi-image theater show; permanent, hands-on and changing exhibit, including an opportunity to see how you would look "riding" Saddlebreds; and a unique gift shop. Open daily 9-5; except November-March, closed Mondays and Tuesdays, and some holidays. Admission.

KENTUCKY
Keenland Association Library
P.O. Box 1690
Lexington, KY 40592-1690
(606) 254-3412   (606) 288-4348 fax
Research and reference facility with an emphasis on the Thoroughbred horse.

KENTUCKY
Kentucky Derby Museum
704 Central Avenue, Gate 1, Churchill Downs
Louisville, KY 40208
(502)637-1111
e-mail: info@derbymuseum.org
Web: http://www.derbymuseum.org
Season: Year-round

See Every Derby, Every Day!
Come see "The Greatest Two Minutes in Sports" at the Kentucky Derby Museum. Visit three floors of fascinating exhibits, tour Churchill Downs, shop in the Finish Line gift shop and enjoy lunch at the Derby Cafe. The Museum is open seven days a week, from 9:00 a.m. to 5:00 p.m. except Thanksgiving, Christmas, Derby Day, and Oaks Days.

KENTUCKY
Kentucky Horse Park 🐎 🛒
4089 Iron Works Pike
Lexington, KY 40511-8434
(606) 259-4231
e-mail: khp@mis.net
Web: www.horseworld.com
Season: Year-round

Located in the heart of the Bluegrass.
The Park is showcased by museums, galleries, theaters, and attractions of more than 45 breeds of horses. Visitors can meet retired racing greats at the prestigious Hall of Champions or view the pageantry of the colorful Parade of Breeds. Whether its camping, horseback riding, a leisurely tour in a carriage or experiencing one of the more than sixty equine special events, a day at the Park is the experience of a lifetime.

NEW MEXICO
Museum of the Horse
Hwy 70 East, P.O. Box 40
Ruidoso Downs, NM 88346
(800)263-5929 or (505)378-4142
Season: Year-round

Home of "Free Spirits at Noisy Water."
One of the world's largest equine sculptures, over three stories high. Features more than 10,000 horse-related items, including wagons, saddles, tack and carriages. Also fine western art, special events and specially scheduled horsemanship demonstrations. Next door to Ruidoso Downs Race Track and Cowboy Riding Stables. Among New Mexico's top museums.

NEW YORK
The Harness Racing Museum and Hall of Fame
240 Main Street
P.O. Box 590
Goshen, NY 10924-0590
(914) 294-6330   (914) 294-3463 fax

Find memorabilia devoted to the Standardbred racing sport. A print and video library. The Hall of Fame honors the outstanding contributors to harness racing, horses, trainers and stables.

OKLAHOMA
National Cowboy Hall of Fame and Western Heritage Center
1700 N.E. 63rd Street
Oklahoma City, OK 73111
(405)478-2250
Season: Year-round Hours; Vary by season, call.
Preserves accurately and authentically the rich heritage of the American West.

OREGON
National Historic Oregon Trail Interpretive Center
Flagstaff Hill, OR Hwy 86
Baker City, OR 97814
(503)523-1845
Season: Year-round, closed holidays
Pioneer life on the Oregon Trail through living history presentations, exhibits and multimedia.

TEXAS
American Quarter Horse Heritage Center and Museum
2601 I-40 E. (Exit 72A)
Amarillo, TX 79104
(888)209-8322   (806) 376-1005 fax
e-mail: AQHA.com//hcm
Web: www.AQHA.com
Season: Year-round
Hours: Vary by season, call.
Information about the breed. The world's most versatile horse...now there's a museum where you can see why. AQHA and AQHYA Members get in FREE.

TEXAS
Cowboy Artists of America Museum
1550 Bandera Hwy
Kerrville, TX 78028
(210)896-2553
Realistic paintings and bronzes of the Cowboy Artists of America preserving the cowboy culture. Collection of the art of contemporary cowboy artists. Special artist programs often scheduled.

VERMONT
The National Museum of the Morgan Horse
P.O. Box 700
Shelburne, VT 05482
(802)985-8665   (802)985-5242 fax
e-mail: national_museum@hotmail.com
Web: members.tripod.com/~NMMH
Season: Year-round   Admission: Free
Morgans have played a vital part in American history. The museum is dedicated to the preservation and presentation of Morgan heritage. Gift catalog available, ornaments, cards, T-shirts, prints...more.

VERMONT
The University of Vermont Morgan Horse Farm
RFD 1
Middlebury, VT 05753
(802)388-2011
Season: May 1-October 31   Hours: 9 - 4 daily
The Morgan Horse... First and oldest of America's light horse breeds. Come learn about the Morgan horse and see outstanding examples of the breed.

VIRGINIA
National Sporting Library
301 West Washington Street
P.O. Box 1335
Middleburg, VA 22117-1335
(703)687-6542
Season: Year-round
Over 11,000 volumes on horses and horse sports. Modern titles and historic dating back to 1528.

WYOMING
Buffalo Bill Historical Center
720 Sheridan Way
Cody, WY 82414
(307)587-4771
http://www.TrueWest.com/BBHC
Season: Year-round, Open daily
One of the world's largest and finest museums devoted to the art, history and culture of the American West.

OVERNIGHT STABLING

NATIONWIDE / USA / CANADA
Equine Travellers of America, Inc.
P.O. Box 322 LJ
Arkansas City, KS 67005-0322
(316)442-8131

Season: Year-round

The Nationwide Overnight Stabling Directory and Equestrian Vacation Guide.
The Original "Stabling Directory of Quality Stabling", published yearly since 1982. Everything needed in planning a trip with your own horses. Stabling facilities available nationwide. Directory serves as a do-it-yourself vacation guide. The Directory makes traveling and vacationing with your horses **easier, more convenient, less troublesome and practically worry free.** Stabling hosts inquiries welcome. $26.95 plus $2.50 handling. Major credit cards accepted.

NATIONWIDE
Horseman's Travel Guide
Audenreed Press
P.O. Box 1305 #103
Brunswick, ME 04011
(207) 833-5016 Orders - (888) 315-0582

Since 1980, this overnight travel guide has listed hundreds of stables, motels, campgrounds, bed & breakfasts, and fairgrounds that cater to all horse hauling travelers. Perfect for horsemen on the road to shows, trail rides, moving and vacations. Updated yearly. $12.95 plus $2.00 postage and handling.

ILLINOIS
Bear Branch Horse Camp
P.O. Box 40, HWY 145
Eddyville, IL 62928
(616)672-4249   (618)672-4739 fax
e-mail: manders@shawnee.link.com
Season open: Year-round   Airport: Nashville, KY
Guest Capacity: 4 cabins, 80 campsites w/hookups, 40 acres of primitive camping

Bear Branch Horse Camp, Outfitter, Log Cabin Restaurant and the Ultimate Trail Ride.
Overlooking Lusk Creek Canyon, one of the most scenic areas in the 275,000 acre Shawnee National Forest. Ride our lush forest trails, ford rocky creeks, travel down rock canyons, circle & climb high bluffs under waterfalls into large caves, you'll see why this is the home of the Ultimate Trail Ride. Featuring a Rustic Log Cabin Restaurant, tack shop, general store, a barn with 40 bedded horse stalls. Heated and air conditioned shower house with laundry facilities, dump station, a 2 acre pond for swimming and fishing, and cabins for rent as well as trail horses. Trail Guide in camp at all times.

NEVADA
Humboldt
County Fairgrounds
1000 Fairgrounds Road
(Mail - 50 W. Winnemucca Blvd.)
Winnemucca, NV 89445
(702) 623-2220
e-mail: sheree@winnemucca.desertlinc.com

Season: Year-round   Guest Capacity: 300 Stalls

In Winnemucca, There's More Than Meets the Eye! Stabling For The Weary Traveller.
Winnemucca and the Humboldt County Fairgrounds welcome travellers with horses passing through
the state of Nevada to stop and rest for a spell. Conveniently located on Interstate 80 and Highway 95,
the Fairgrounds has over 300 stalls available for rent. Covered pens and barns are $10.00 per animal
per night. No tie-ups please. *Remember in Winnemucca, there's more than meets the eye!*

OREGON
Black Butte Stables
13892 Hawksbeard Road, P.O. Box 8000
Black Butte Ranch, OR 97759-8000
(541)595-2061   Fax: 541-595-6053
e-mail: blackbuttestables.com

Season: Daily, Memorial Day to Labor Day, weekends year-round
Guest capacity: 40 or more by prior arrangement.

View the Cascade Mountains of Central Oregon from Horseback.
Knowledgeable guides lead you through Aspen and Pine groves and across creeks on the 1/2 hour,
1-1/2 hour, 2 hour, half day and all day adventure rides. Try one of our meal rides featuring a hearty
western breakfast, or an authentic western barbecue. Tell us what you would like to see and we will
put together a ride that will be the highlight of your visit to Central Oregon. Horse boarding is available
for those traveling with horses. We have pony rides for the young buckaroos, and western riding
lessons too.

SOUTH DAKOTA
Two Bar T Ranch
HCR 30, Box 13
Spearfish, SD 57783
(605) 578-2438

Season: Year-round   Airport: Rapid City, SD   Guest Capacity: 6

Bring Your Own Horse to Ride the Ranch and Black Hills Trails.
Come vacation in our newly restored fully furnished log cabin located on a working cattle ranch. The
ranch sits on the northern edge of the beautiful Black Hills in Western South Dakota. Our cabin sleeps
up to 3 couples. Come alone or bring your friends. Comfortable lodging, plenty of riding and lots to
do. We are only 8 miles from historic Deadwood, the wild west town that offers gambling, skiing, and
snowmobiling. We have large corrals and 4 indoor stalls for your horses.

Tell the site that you found them through the Horse Lovers Vacation Guide.

Wilderness Pack Trips & Backcountry Base Camps Provide the Ultimate Horseback Travel Vacation

No two pack trips are ever the same...you see things that you might not have noticed any other way

If you love horses and nature, there is nothing like it. You depend on your horse for everything. No two pack trips are ever the same, even if you go with the same outfitter. Why? Every time you ride out for a week your senses open up to see things that you might not have ever noticed. Each trip brings it's own set of new experiences, wildlife sightings, weather and new people to share them with. Contact a professional outfitter for a tour of his special country.

My first pack trip with a professional outfitter, was in 1975. I had never tent camped before. My friends said they thought it might be fun but for one reason or another couldn't make it. I was determined...and a little nervous about going all by myself. "This will make me a better person," I thought, "to endure the hardships of life on the trail". I found the trip to be comfortable, great meals, good horses and wonderful companions. Pack trips are one of the best for singles as you immediately find yourself in a group. You don't need to provide your own. If it is a group made up of horse people you have much to talk about around the campfire – the horses back home.

Since then I have ridden out on more than 40 pack trips. I still get a feeling of excitement as I pack up my duffel. What will I see? Lots of wildlife? Will it rain? There still is that moment as I step out from a warm cabin, into the chill of the high country morning, when I think, "Gosh it's cold, I'm really going to freeze". When you are camping out in nature, the temperatures never seem as extreme as when you leave the warmth of a building. If you are outfitted correctly even temperatures in the 30's don't seem too bad. Rainy trips are sometimes the best as everyone opens up with a little adversity.

Every part of the country has beautiful natural areas, they are all different. There is always something new to see. More than one time I have marvelled at the morning dew dancing on the wildflowers. Or enjoyed the soothing sounds of a babbling brook outside my tent, awakened to the hoot of an owl, snort of a elk, howl of the coyote or even the chomping of the horses grazing just outside my tent. Only inches away.

Many people say to me that they don't want to try a pack trip as they usually ride along at a walk only. There is a lot more excitement to a pack trip than galloping horses. There is something so special about getting back in 25 or so miles away from the nearest civilization. Carrying all of your camping gear over steep and narrow trails, it is not condusive to moving on into a trot or canter. Even so, some of the most exciting riding experiences I have had have been on pack trips. Taking horses where I never dreamed horses could go – at the walk.

If you have never packed in before take at least a 5 day trip, 7 would be better. It takes a couple of days to adjust to this lifestyle. Once you have you won't want it to end.

PACK TRIPS & BASE CAMPS

Ah Wilderness!! The best way to see the backcountry is from the back of a good horse. There are basically two types of back country trips. Those that have moving camps where all supplies and gear are taken in by pack string– pack trips, and those that are permanent – base camps. These take their guests into a camp that is already preset.

ALASKA – Pack Trips
Southfork Outfit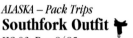
HC 03, Box 8485
Mile 110 Glenn Hwy
Palmer, AK 99645
(907)746-4290

Season: Year -round
Airport: Ankorage

Year-round, All-round, Outdoor Outfit.
Guided horsepack expeditions and hunts, 3-21 day tours. Located on Sheep Mountain Game Reserve, explore the alpine glaciers of the Chugach Mountains and the nostalgic hills of the Talkeetnas. Wildlife observation and photography in a casual western Alaskan lifestyle. Write for rates, dates and our FREE Brochure. We can put together a customized adventure for your group.

ARIZONA – Base Camps
Don Donnelly
Horseback Vacations
6010 S. Kings Ranch Road
Gold Canyon, AZ 81529
(602) 982-8895 or 1-800-346-4403
Web: www.arizonaguide.com/dondonnelly

Season: March-Nov.   Guest Capacity: 13-30

Our Goal for Our Guests:
Adventure! Fun! Excitement!
Spectacular Arizona riding locations: 3-8 day vacations. Monument Valley with it's giant monoliths or the serenity of the White Mountains, the diversity of Arizona can offer something for everyone's state of mind. We provide all your equipment and well trained horses. All you need bring is a desire for the vacation of a lifetime. Call or fax for free information about the different possibilities.

84

CALIFORNIA – Pack Trips
Frontier Pack Trains 🐎

Summer Address:
June- September
Star Rt 3, Box 18
June Lake, CA 93529
(619) 648-7701

Winter Address:
October - May
2095 Van Loon
Bishop, CA 93514
(760) 873-7971

Season: June - September   Airport: Reno, NV

Ride Yosemite National Park and the Ansel Adams Wilderness.
Explore the uncrowded back country and revel in the beauty of the Sierras. We put together a first class ride including good mountain horses, tents and camping gear, delicious meals, and experienced guide service. Join us on moving back country pack trips 3 to 9 nine days in length, spring and fall horse drives, and Mustang observation. Learn from our mountain horsemanship courses emphasizing wilderness etiquette, horse use, pack equipment and vet care.

CALIFORNIA – Pack Trips
Red's Meadow Pack Station
& Agnew Meadows Pack Station 🐎

P.O. Box 395
Mammoth Lakes, CA 93546
(800)292-7758 (760) 934-2345 - summer
(760)873-3928 - winter
Web: http://www.mammothweb.com/redsmeadow

Season: Mid-June to Mid-October
Airport: Reno, NV

The Eastern High Sierra is the "Hidden Treasure" of California.
Trail rides and pack trips into Yosemite National Park and the Ansel Adams / Minaret Wilderness as well as the John Muir Wilderness and Sequoia King National Park. Over 100 lakes and miles of streams available in some of the finest scenery of the High Sierra. 40 years of providing quality service. Many interesting loop trips of various duration.

CALIFORNIA – Pack Trips
Rock Creek Pack Station 🐎 🖼

P.O. Box 248
Bishop, CA 93515
(760) 872-8331

Season: May - October
Airport: Reno and Las Vegas, NV

Ride the Pacific Crest Trail.
Explore the Pacific Crest, through the John Muir Wilderness, Kings Canyon, Sequoia or Yosemite National Parks. A variety of scheduled trips explore the most scenic areas. Ride through steep walled canyons, top high passes, fish at pristine lakes, pass cascading waterfalls. Over 40 years in the outfitting business. Well-run trips, good equipment, hearty meals, experienced guides and trail-wise horses. Spring and Fall horse drives and field courses on the Mustang. See this photo in color on page 1.

CANADA – Alberta – Pack Trips & Base Camps
Holiday on Horseback 🐴
Box 2280
Banff, AB, T0L 0C0 CANADA
(800)661-8352 or (403)762-4551
e mail: warner@horseback.com

Season: May-October   Airport: Calgary, AB   Guest Capacity: 4-20

The Ultimate Horseback Adventures in Banff National Park.
Ride the Cascade Valley Range for a mountain wilderness experience you will never forget, absolutely gorgeous country. A variety of trips available from 3 to 6 days. Your guides, saddle horses, cooks, packers, delicious meals and back-country tenting accommodations included. Prices begin around $95 U.S. per day. Both camps and moving pack trips available. Or if you wish the joy of riding through the wilderness without camping. Enjoy nature's best at Sundance and Halfway Lodges from overnight to 6 days. Nature study packages.

CANADA – British Columbia – Pack Trips
Rainbow Mountain Outfitting 🐴
Box 3066
Anaheim Lake, BC V0L 1C0   Canada
(604) 742-3539

Season: July-September
Guest Capacity: 10
Airport: Anaheim Lake via Vancouver

Wilderness Adventure in British Columbia's Largest Wilderness Park – Tweedsmuir.
Completely outfitted 6-10 day wilderness adventures in Tweedsmuir Park's Rainbow Mountains. David Dorsey, descended from native ancestors and pioneers, brings generations of mountain experience to a first class vacation. Gourmet meals are a trademark. Most of the riding is done above timberline with magnificent views of the glacial clad coast range contrasted with the colorful volcanic Rainbow Mountains and wildflowers.

COLORADO – Base Camps
Old Glendevey Ranch 🐴
Glendevey Colorado Route
3219 County Rd. 190
Jelm, WY 82063
(800)807-1444
e-mail: glendevey@aol.com
Web: www.duderanch.org/glendevey

Season: May to November
Guest capacity: 18
Airport: Laramie, WY   Weekly stays

A True Wilderness Experience.
We are a small family run guest ranch that offers a charming, warm setting with all the traditional activities of a guest ranch. We "specialize" in saddle horse and pack mule pack trips to our 10,000' Rawah Wilderness base camp. Comfortable camp with showers, wall tents, cots and amenities not often found in the backcountry. There you may fish the high lakes & beaver ponds, ride and enjoy the surrounding beauty. "A wonderful way to rough it," comfortably.

Packing For The Trail, What To Take?

*Pack Right...
Go Light into
the Forest.
Take only
what you
really need.*

Vacation time is here, but what should you take along? If you are about to ride off on a pack trip the best thought is to pack light. Always check with your outfitter to find out what temperatures you will encounter. The higher the altitude the chillier the nights. A general rule is that temperatures drop about 4 degrees for every thousand feet you climb. So just because it is August and 95 degrees at 7,500' where the trail starts, don't expect that to be true at 13,000'. Take appropriate clothing that can be worn in layers. Expect to wear your clothing for several days, not a new outfit each day. A pack trip is not a fashion show.

Packing your gear.

Pack all of your clothing in a side zippered, canvas or nylon duffel. A duffle should not weigh over 30 lbs. You should get all of your personal belongings into one duffel. If your bedroll is bulky it may go as a second duffel if the outfitter agrees to two. Don't get too large a duffel as a half filled duffel is floppy and hard for the packer to secure on the pack animals.

To keep your things organized, as well as dry inside your duffel, pack all of your clothing in plastic bags with wire ties. If you collect several colors of plastic bags, one for underwear, one for shirts and jeans and another for toiletries, you will know at a glance which holds the dry socks!

When packing medicines, only take enough for your trip. Transfer them to unbreakable bottles or pill tins. There should be nothing in your duffel that is breakable as a lot of pressure is applied by the ropes that secure the packs to the pack stock. Reverse the batteries in your flashlight so that it won't be accidently turned on while jostling along on the trail. It is dark in the back country and there are no electric lights.

What should go on your horse?

Anything you need during the day should be secured to your saddle. Your slicker and jacket can tie directly on the saddle. If you have saddle bags, and the outfitter allows them, you might be wise to bring your own. When filling your saddlebags weigh them ahead of time so that both sides are the same weight. This will help keep your horse from getting sore from an uneven load.

Cameras, film, binoculars, suntan lotion, canteen, drinking cup, and any breakables you carry, should be carried in your saddlebags. If you bring breakables, pack them inside a plastic or leather container that will contain any splinters should articles break.

Staying dry.

While we always hope for a dry trip, it is not always possible. Sometimes the rainy trips are more fun as the adversity opens up the riders to new experiences. Groups tend to get to know each other better when they have something to laugh about. You will need a good riding slicker. Even if your trip is in the desert. Don't rely on a cheap poncho. Ponchos are so light weight that they have several drawbacks. One, if you do have a rainy trip they may not last the whole trip. Putting them on and taking them off, stuffing them in saddle bags, will take their toll. Two, when it is windy they blow away from you allowing you to be wet. Three, they drain down your front and allow water to run to the deepest part of your saddle, where you sit! Finally, loose Ponchos scare horses.

If you decide to be stylish with an Australian Outback, make sure it is waterproof. They all aren't. The recommended type are the good old yellow riding slickers that cover you and your saddle from shoulders to foot. They are inexpensive and do the trick.

Warm waterproofed leather gloves, a waterproof hat cover and boot rubbers are a good investment too. Boot rubbers keep your boots dry from the morning dew even if it doesn't rain.

Clothing

The mountains are beautiful but you need to be prepared for different temperatures. Wear clothing that combines in layers. At high altitude bring a warm winter jacket for evenings around the campfire. Take enough to be comfortable, plus one extra change of underwear.

Most outfitters provide tents for double occupancy. Keep in mind if you are joining alone, you may have a roommate. Sleepwear varies, you need to seek your own comfort. Always change from what you are wearing during the day. Your normal daily perspiration is trapped in your clothing, as your body cools down it will cause you to feel chilly if you don't. Some people like to bring jogging suits, others long underwear and a ski cap to sleep in. Remember you loose most of your warmth through your head. If it is sticking out of your sleeping bag you may be cold.

Bedrolls

When you are on a high altitude trip, it can be cold at night. You will need a 4-season rated bag. Get one that is rated at least 10 degrees below your lowest intended temperature. You can always unzip them to be cooler. It's better to be safe. Down-filled or fiberfill is personal preference. If you find yourself cold at night, ask your outfitter if he has an extra packing tarp to put over your bag. This will supplement your warmth. Don't use plastic or the silver emergency blankets for this purpose. They don't breathe, condensation, will collect on the underside and rain back down on you.

If your outfitter doesn't provide a mattresses for you, look for a Thermarest pad. This is a combination foam pad and air mattress. You unroll them, open the air valve, and it takes in air. You might want to give a few extra puffs of air to get the right firmness. Make sure it is full length for comfort. Or if you can roll it tightly, a 3 or 4 inch thick foam pad makes a great comfy bed. But it is bulky to pack and absorbs water should your tent leak. Cots are not as warm as cold air is allowed to flow under you. When you have a mattress on the ground you are warmer.

Large pillows are too bulky to pack. They make small camping pillows if you wish. The most space saving method is to just pack a pillow case. Fold your down jacket so that the zipper is inside and stuff that pillowcase to make your pillow.

Bathing

Many outfitters provide solar showers set off from camp. Others ask you to depend on sponge baths. Take biodegradable soaps along for washing. Then only use them at least 200 feet away from streams and lakes. Remember, you are a guest in this wilderness paradise. The creatures who live here depend upon that water to drink. Don't make those downstream from your bathing hole sick. Heat water over the fire, carry it off to your tent or a secluded spot in a small bucket or wash basin, then wash.

Each outfitter has their own latrine system. Most provide a latrine tent in camp. Others just a shovel with a roll of toilet paper. Make sure you take along packets of tissue along for use on the trail.

Pack right. Have fun on the trail

The best vacations are spent on the back of a good horse. If you love horses, and nature, there is no vacation quite as wonderful as a wilderness pack trip. You can be very comfortable on the trail. Just think ahead of time what you really need. Ask your outfitter for a list of what to take along, and what temperatures you will encounter. Don't over pack. Take no more than you think you will need. We can always tell the novice camper because they take too much. Pack for comfort, but pack light.

COLORADO – Pack Trips
Schmittel Packing
& Outfitting

15206 Hwy 285 - L
Saguache, CO 81149
reservations: (330) 659-6007

Season: June-September
Guest capacity: 7-8
Airport: Alamosa, CO

**True Wilderness Adventure
for Avid Trail Riders.**

Ride deep into the Weminuche, La Garita or Sangre de Cristo Wilderness areas. Hundreds of miles of scenic trail. Colorado's largest wilderness. Gorgeous 14,000' snow-capped peaks give riders long views over a hundred miles from the top. Thousands of elk, deer, coyotes, bighorn and more. Moving camps are not used more than once a year. Each trip is to a different area, customized to the wishes of the group. Hearty meals. Horses that ride like privately owned mounts. Book early as many riders return yearly, some will be back for their 21st! 3,5, and 7 day trips. Colorado outfitters registration #344.

COLORADO – Pack Trips
Weminuche
Wilderness Adventures

17754 County Road 501
Bayfield, CO 81122
(970)884-2555 summer
(602)471-0065 winter

Season: June - September
Airport: Durango, CO
Guest Capacity: 4-8.

**The Weminuche on Horseback –
Truly the Experience of a Lifetime!**

Return to the joys and exhilarations of a lost way of life on a pack trip into the wilderness area of the San Juan Mountains. On this exciting adventure we reach deep into majestic mountain back country, comfortably mounted on well-trained horses, being outdoors for every part of every day where land and nature are still peaceful and free. Colorado outfitters registration #390.

COLORADO – Pack Trips
Wit's End Guest Ranch & Resort

254 County Road 500
Bayfield, CO 81122
(970)884-4113 v

Spring - Arizona Desert and Mountain Ride
Summer - Weminuche Wilderness Continental Divide Ride

Season: June-October   Guest capacity: 5-12   Airport: Durango, LaPlata, CO

Pack Trips to Take You Throughout the 600,000 acre Weminuche Wilderness.
We have 12 different camps for our riders. Spend 1 to 7 nights in one or more locations. Trips are on horseback and will take you to the most spectacular mountain country you will see anywhere. Many of Colorado's famous 14,000' peaks. Loads of lakes, creeks and game. Also a continental divide ride is offered. Pack trips run June through October. See also "Hunting/Fishing Guides" and pages 4 and 5 for color photos.

MEXICO – Pack Trips
Saddling South
Baja Pack Trips ⊺
P.O. Box 827
Calistoga, CA 94515
(800)398-6200
(707) 942-4550 phone/fax
e-mail: tourbaja@iname.com
web: www.tourbaja.com
Season: October-May
Guest Capacity: 3-8
Airport: Loreto, or Baja California Sur,
     Mexico. Airport pickup available.

Grab Your Sombrero for an Incredible Journey, into the Heart of the Sierra Giganta.
Saddling South takes you along volcanic ridges, through cactus garden valleys and into the lush palm springs in Baja's spectacular desert mountains. Owner Trudi Angell, with 20 years experience exploring this magnificent peninsula, offers a chance to learn traditions and histories of the remote ranching lifestyle unique to Baja, Mexico. Join us as our local guides share their wisdom and lore along the original missionary trails of the Californias.

MONTANA – Pack Trips
JJJ Wilderness Ranch ⊺
Box 310 - R
Augusta, MT 59410
(406)562-3653   (406)562-3836 fax
e-mail:triplej@3rivers.net
Web: www.triplejranch.com

Season: June - September   Guest capacity: 8   Airport: Great Falls, MT
Fully-outfitted Trips Into the Famous Bob Marshall Wilderness.

Let the JJJ Wilderness Ranch introduce you into the world of pristine wilderness. Fully outfitted, your trip into this magnificent, unspoiled country is a four-star adventure. Our quality horses are mountain savvy and will take you deep into the back country to view wildlife and gorgeous scenery. These limited trips average 8 guests for 5 to 8 days at a time and will be an experience like no other.

MONTANA – Pack Trips
Monture Face Outfitters ⊺ 🐴
Box 27 Clearwater Junction
Greenough, MT 59836
(888)420-5768
Web: www.montanaoutfitter.com
Season: June to September   Guest capacity: 12   Airport: Missoula, MT

Your Host's to the "Bob Marshall Wilderness", 1.5 Million acres of Pristine Beauty.
Travel into and through the wilderness on top notch horses and mules. Pack trips are flexible, from 3 days to a high adventure 10 day roving experience. Wildflowers and wildlife are abundant providing photo opportunities at every bend of the trail and the trout fishing is outstanding. Only the highest quality ingredients are used in our gourmet wilderness kitchen. Build campfires at night and immerse yourself in a sea of stars. We have one ultimate goal: to share the magic of wilderness. Knowledgeable, experienced and quality oriented.

MONTANA – Pack Trips
Seven Lazy P Ranch Outfitters 🐎
P.O. Box 178
Choteau, MT 59422
(406)466-2044
Season: May-November
Airport: Great Falls, MT
Guest capacity: 10

**The Bob Marshall Wilderness,
Over a Million Acres to Explore.**
Well outfitted trips through some of the most outstanding wilderness country in America. Ride the Continental Divide, view the Chinese Wall. Great mountain horses, comfortable camps, outstanding meals and a lot of time in the saddle. Outstanding fishing plentiful wildlife - Mule and whitetail deer, Rocky Mountain goats, Bighorn sheep, moose, black bear, golden eagles, grouse and songbirds greatly add to your pleasure.

MONTANA _ Pack Trips
WTR Outfitters, Inc. 🐎
520 Cooper Lake Rd
Ovando, MT 59854
(800)WTR-5666 or
(406)793-5666 phone/fax

Season: June-December
Airport: Missoula, MT
Guest capacity: 6 - 20

**Providing Horseback Adventures For
Everyone Since 1940.**
Adventure on horseback into the Bob
Marshall Wilderness complex with over 1200 miles of trails. View wildlife, birds and flowers, fish backcountry waters, explore ice caves and the Chinese Wall. Learn new skills in horsemanship and survival. Experience an excellent camp and marvelous meals. Everyone is welcome, singles, families on our 3 to 10 day roving summer pack trips.

OREGON – Pack Trips
Black Butte Stables 🐎
13892 Hawksbeard Road
P.O. Box 8000
Black Butte Ranch, OR 97759-8000
(541)595-2061Web: www.oregoncowboy.com

Season: Memorial Day - Labor Day & weekends year-round
Guest capacity: 15
Airport: Redmond or Bend, OR

Discover the Spectacular Beauty of Oregon's Cascade Wilderness by Horseback.
Experienced guides lead you through miles of Aspen, Cedar and Ponderosa Pine forests, across sparkling creeks, and into the fresh mountain air of the Three Sisters, Mt. Jefferson, and Mt. Washington Wilderness areas. Choose from custom designed Full Service Pack Trips (gear, food, cooks, guide, wranglers, pack animals and saddle horses included), Drop Camps, and Wilderness Adventure Rides. Join us for the experience of a lifetime.

SOUTH DAKOTA – Pack Trips
Dakota Badland Outfitters 🐎
P.O. Box 85
Custer, SD 57730
(605)673-5363
Web: www.wordpros.com/dakota

Season: May 15 to October 8   Guest capacity: 2 - 10
Airport: Rapid City Regional Airport

Ride the Remote Badlands National Park or the Black Hills National Forest.
This authentic working horse ranch offers horseback expeditions into the remote Badlands National Park, and the Black Hills National Forest. Experience the back country of the Dakota territory with a top notch pack trip or ranch style base camp. Emphasis is placed on long rides and good horsemanship. The Dakota bred horses are active and alert, a pleasure to ride in this ruggedly beautiful country. These trips are highly rated, references available.

UTAH – Pack Trips
Best Western Ruby's Inn Outlaw Trail Rides 🐎
P.O. Box 17
Bryce, UT 84764
(800)468-8660
Web : www.rubysinn.com

Season: April-October
Guest capacity: 20
Airport: Bryce, UT

Bryce Canyon National Park and the Famous Outlaw Trails.
Our Best Western Lodge is located next to Bryce Canyon National Park in southern Utah. Ride along the famous Outlaw Trails once traveled by Butch Cassidy and his wild bunch. Experience this unique red rock country, high in the Dixie National Forest. Narrow canyons remain much the same as when first seen by pioneers. Enjoy 1 and 2 hour rides as well as 1/2 day and all day tours. Our lodge has 369 guest rooms, pool, spas, nightly rodeos and western activities. Horse boarding available.

TRAIL COURTESY
In the backcountry, say hello! A little simple courtesy makes life more pleasant for everyone. Observe the basics of trail courtesy:

In steep, rough country, down-hill traffic usually yields to uphill traffic. If you have a better place to pull off, do so, and let the other folks pass through.

People with llamas, on foot, or on mountain bikes should yield to stock traffic because it is easier for them to move off the trail. If they don't, smile and yield the way, or ask them to stand below the trail and wait quietly for your stock to pass.– *Courtesy, U.S. Forest Service*

UTAH – Base Camps
Hondoo Rivers & Trails
P.O. Box 98 - HLVG
Torrey, UT 84775

(800)33CANYONS ask for Lyn
Web: www.hondoo.com

Season: May-October
Airport: Grand Junction, CO   Guest capacity: 15

Marvel at the Petroglyphs, Indian Ruins and Rock Formations.
On horseback explore the beautiful red rock canyon country of Capitol Reef National Park. During summer's heat climb the cool green Henry Mountains, average temperature 78 degrees, or enjoy the warmth of the desert spring and fall. Ride out on photographic wildlife safaris, elk, buffalo, antelope, or wild horses. Study ancient Indian petroglyphs, join a rock art seminar. Everything is included. Good Quarter horses, camping gear, well-prepared meals and knowledgeable guide service.

VIRGINIA – Pack Trips
Virginia Mountain Outfitters
Rt 1, Box 244
Buena Vista, VA 24416
(540)261-1910

Season: April-November   Airport: Roanoke, VA

3, 4, and 5 Day Blue Ridge Pack Trips.
Virginia Mountain Outfitters is a full-service trail riding operation. We offer everything from half day and all day rides to overnights and multi-day pack trips. Bed and Breakfast packages and 5 day mountain Inn to Inn rides. We feature small personal groups and love families! Near historic Lexington and the Virginia Horse Center.

WASHINGTON – Pack Trips
Cascade Wilderness Outfitters
P.O. Box 103
Carlton, WA 98814
(509)997-0155

Season: June 15-October 31   Guest capacity: 4-5   Airport: Wenachee, WA

The Beautiful "Pasayten" and "Lake Chelan Sawtooth Wilderness".
Enjoy all that the beautiful Cascades have to offer, the plush green valleys, alpine meadows and the snow-capped peaks. Rely on our trail wise horses and mules to take your family and friends across the wilderness. You'll ride to scenic locations and nearby lakes. Hiking, fishing, photography, and evenings of stimulating conversation around the campfire with dutch oven dinners.
Trips available – deluxe, standard, drop camps, fall hunting and day rides.

English Riding   Western Riding   Take Your Own Horse

WYOMING – Pack Trips
Boulder Lake Lodge

P.O. Box 1100- HL
Pinedale, WY 82941
(800)788-5401 or (307)537-5400

Season: Mid-June to Mid-September
Airport: Jackson Hole, WY
Guest capacity: 6

Ride the Winds!
Well outfitted pack trips into Wyoming's
scenic Wind River Mountain Range. You will
traverse the remote high mountain trails along the Continental Divide on one of our deluxe, all-accommodation included trips. See country that is unchanged since the fur trapping and Mountain Man era. Reasonably priced package trips for family or exclusive groups.

WYOMING – Pack Trips
Green River Outfitters

P.O. Box 727
Pinedale, WY 82941
(307)367-2416

Season: May to October   Guest capacity: 8
Airport: Jackson Hole, WY

**Unique Horseback Riding Adventures in the Bridger-Teton National Forest
and Gros Ventre Wilderness Areas.**
For a real taste of the "Old West" away from crowds, combined with good mountain horses, experienced guides, spectacular mountain scenery, and lots of wildlife photo opportunities, come give us a visit! We offer pack trips, day rides, overnight "Bed and Breakfast' type rides, stream and lake fishing, float trips, and just plain fun and relaxation. Historic log cabin and deluxe wall-tent accommodations.

WYOMING – Pack Trips
Yellowstone Institute

P.O. Box 117
Yellowstone National Park, WY 82190
(307)344-2294 (307)344-2485 fax

e-mail: dkline@yellowstoneassociation.org
Web: www.yellowstoneassociation.org

Season: June to September
Guest capacity: 8 to 14 per trip
Airport: Bozeman, MT Jackson Hole, WY

Educational Pack Trips Inside Yellowstone National Park.
The Yellowstone Institute is a non-profit field school operated in partnership with the National Park Service. We offer affordable 3-day, 4-day, and 5-day pack trips with emphasis on natural history, cultural history, and minimum impact camping. Join us for a unique educational experince in a spectacular wilderness setting. Please call or write for our free catalog.

WYOMING – Pack Trips
Yellowstone Outfitters 🐴
Fishing & Sightseeing Pack Trips
Box 1156 - R
Afton, WY 83110
(800)447-4711 or (307) 886-9693
Fax: 307-886-5284

Season; June-August
Airport: Jackson Hole, WY
Guest Capacity: 8-12

**Teton Wilderness Pack Trips,
an Orvis Endorsed Flyfishing camp.**

Deluxe 6 day horseback pack-in fly fishing on the head waters of the Yellowstone and Thorofare Rivers, in the most remote area of the Teton Wilderness. Abundant wildlife. Fish for trophy Cutthrout Trout. (3-4lbs) 6 day or longer moving horse pack trips for private groups. Deluxe tent camps with excellent full course meals. Experienced cooks, guides and packers included.

Pack Trip Tips:

When packing your flashlight, always take the batteries out and reverse them. This will prevent the light from accidentally being turned on from the movement of the pack animals on the trail. There are no electric lights in the backcountry.

If you find yourself without a flashlight, make sure that you arrange your bedroll and your night clothes in a way that you can locate them by touch. Then you can still have an enjoyable trip even without light...and more of an adventure!

Wildlife can be seen most often in the early morning and evening at dusk. When riding out early in the morning ride silently so as not to surprise them long before you can see them.

Rise early in the morning and look out into the meadow where the horses are grazing. Often deer, elk, or mountain sheep may be seen nearby. Take your camera and hike away from camp before breakfast or just before sunset to see wildlife.

Changing temperatures can zap the strength out of aging batteries. Start out with new camera batteries. Don't forget to take plenty of film!

RENTAL CABINS

Create your own vacation. Get away to a secluded spot where you have your own vacation home, a place for your horses, and lots of trails to explore.

ILLINOIS
Hideout Cabin 🐎

Mailing Address:
111 S. McVicker Drive
Energy, IL 62933
(618)942-3880   (618)942-2168 fax

Ride Scenic Southern Illinois.
Located "back to back" to the Shawnee National Forest, riders have direct access to abundant riding trails right at their doorstep. Explore trails to caves, boulders, and canyons created by the 1800's earthquake. Ride on your own or hire a trail guide. Then return to our fully furnished cabin, television, 2 baths, firepit & gas grill, and small fishing lake. There are limited stalls and pens for your horses. Campers welcome also. Very relaxing, the perfect "*hideout*".

MONTANA
DJ Bar Ranch
and Guest House 🐎

5155 Round Mountain Road
Belgrade, MT 59714
(406)388-7463

Season: Year-round

Come Visit Montana and Enjoy the Big Sky Country in a New Log Home.
Relax under the stars in your own private hot tub. There are many trail heads located within easy day trip distances in the surrounding mountain ranges including Yellowstone National Park, with spectacular destinations and alpine lake fishing. Spanish Peaks is a wilderness area with majestic views of craggy peaks. Treasure the panoramic views of the Gallatin Valley. Rich western decor accents this luxury home with its three bedrooms, two baths, and satellite TV. The kitchen is complete with everything needed to prepare your own meals; or, you may choose to savor one of the area's many fine restaurants.

OHIO
McNutt Farm II Bed & Barn 🐎

6120 Cutler Lake Road
Blue Rock, OH 43720
(740) 674-4555
Season: Year-round   Guest capacity: 20   Airport: Columbus, OH

Bring Your Own Horse and Rent Our Private Log Cabin in Ohio's Hill Country.
Horseman and non-horsemen alike are welcome in our cabin with full kitchen and modern amenities. Roomy box stalls for horses. In the Blue Rock State Park hill country. Near many other state park trail systems within a short drive. Also a program for learning with our horse assist program for riders and carriage drivers. We can help you and your horse get over problems of the trail.

OHIO
Palmerosa Horse Camp & Cabins 🐴

19217 Keifel Road
Laurelville, OH 43135
(614)385-3799
Season: Year-round   Airport: Columbus, OH

**Rent our Bunkhouses or Cabins and Ride
Your Horse Through the Breathtaking Hocking Hills.**
Ride in caves and box canyons, see waterfalls and large rock formations. Our scenic tall hills and deep forests will convince you that southern Ohio is not just flat farmland! Write for literature on our annual organized rides (see "Annual Trail Rides" for dates). Open year-round. Electric and non-electric hookups, well shaded campsites, showers, bunkhouses and cabins.

OKLAHOMA
Tickled Pink Ranch 🏇🐴

HC 15, Box 2020
Smithville, OK 74957
(580)244-3729 phone / fax
Season: June to December   Airport: Ft. Smith

Discover the Kiamichi Mountains of Southeastern Oklahoma.
Come enjoy trail riding on your favorite horse or ours. Ride through tall pine forests, mountain trails, creek crossings and old logging roads. See what nature has to offer from the back of a horse. Our log cabins with a fully furnished kitchen, are nestled on a creek bank. Or bring your camper along, we have lots of shaded parking, clean shower house, hookups, horse stalls and corrals. Enjoy 150 miles of marked trails. Map available or guided riding. Cafes and evening entertainment in town.

SOUTH DAKOTA
Two Bar T Ranch
HCR 30, Box 13
Spearfish, SD 57783
(605)578-2438

Season: Year-round   Airport: Rapid City, SD   Guest Capacity: 6

Bring Your Own Horse to Ride the Ranch and Black Hills Trails.
Come vacation in our newly restored fully furnished log cabin located on a working cattle ranch. The ranch sits on the northern edge of the beautiful Black Hills in Western South Dakota. Our cabin sleeps up to 3 couples. Come alone or bring your friends. Comfortable lodging, plenty of riding and lots to do. We are only 8 miles from historic Deadwood, the wild west town that offers gambling, skiing, and snowmobiling. We have large corrals and 4 indoor stalls for your horses.

TENNESSEE
Gilbertson's Lazy Horse Retreat
938 Schoolhouse Gap Road
Townsend, TN 37882
(423)448-6810

Season: Year-round   Guest capacity: 20   Airport: Knoxville, TN

Take Your Horse On A Memorable Vacation.
Bring your horses to a lovely country setting within the Great Smoky Mountains. We offer a stable with roomy box stalls, exercise paddocks, and three furnished cabins with kitchen, jacuzzi and fireplace in each. Our guests can ride from a variety of trailheads into the Great Smoky Mountains National Park and enjoy the many miles of trails. Beautiful mountain views. Open all year. Our job is helping you create wonderful memories!

WYOMING
Pole Creek Ranch
P.O. Box 278
Pinedale, WY 82941   (307)367-4433
Season: Year round   Airport: Jackson, WY

Relive the Charm of the Old West.
Come stay in our rustic log home while your horses enjoy our 7 acre pasture, corrals and stalls. Horse riding trips into the Wind River Mountains for scenery, camping and fishing are available also. The Wind River Mountains offer 600 miles of trails and 1300 lakes. Ride then relax in the hot tub.

RESORTS

Enjoy the luxury of a full service resort with many activities for the whole family including a good riding program for the equestrians in your family or group. Something for everyone, the riders and non-riders in your group.

ALASKA
Northland Ranch & Resort ⊺

P.O. Box 2376
Kodiak, AK 99615
(907) 486-5578
Season: Year-round   Airport: Ankorage, AK

Scenic, Spectacular Alaska.
Come join us in our comfortable lodge on a cattle and horse ranch. Located in a scenic valley right on the Bay. We offer unlimited horseback riding, world class salmon fishing and wildlife habitat. Our great food and cozy lounge provide relaxing evenings, while days are your own. Advanced to beginner riding and instruction for all ages, lends to an informal vacation.

CALIFORNIA
Alisal Guest Ranch & Resort ⊺

1054 Alisal Road
Solvang, CA 93463
(800)425-4725 or (805)688-6411
Season: Year-round   Guest capacity: 200

Journey Back to the Old West.   Airport: Santa Barbara, CA
Find 10,000 acres of scenic trails for riders of all levels. Saddle up with our experienced wranglers for a breakfast ride to an historic adobe camp. Gallop through oak-shaded valleys to our private lake. Venture out with your own guide to explore the quiet grandeur of our wide open spaces. Special children's riding program. Rodeos and cattle drives for groups. See page 6.

COLORADO
Wit's End
Guest Ranch & Resort ⊺

254 County Road 500
Bayfield, CO 81122
(970)884-4113
Season: Year-round   Guest capacity: 80   Airport: Durango, LaPlata

Historic Wit's End Ranch, Founded in 1859.
Situated in a narrow valley surrounded by 12,000 and 14,000 ft. peaks adjacent to Vallecito Lake (6 miles long). Luxury class log cabins and fine dining in our 125 year old lodge. Enjoy mountain, lake and high country riding with our 100 horses, rodeo arena, full children's program, pack trips, horse and cattle drives, fly-fishing, 50' heated pool, hot tubs, tennis, biking, guided hiking, 4-wheel drive trips. Winter, cross country skiing, snow trail on horseback, snowmobiling, pond skating and sleigh rides. Ranked as one of the country's 12 best by Country Inns Magazine and featured in <u>Elegant Hotels</u>. Please see color photos on pages 4 and 5.

COSTA RICA

Jinetes de Osa Beach and Rainforest Retreat 🐴

P.O. Box 833
Conifer, CO 80433
(303)838-0969 or (800)317-0333
e-mail: crventur@costaricadiving.com   Web: www.costaricadiving.com
Season: Year-round   Airport: San Jose, CR   Guest capacity: 18

World Class Diving and Rain Forest Adventures
Jinetes de Osa offers spectacular expeditions to secluded waterfalls and locations so deep within the surrounding rain forest that they are only accessible atop the most sure footed steed. From your mount you will have access to all the wondrous flora and fauna that makes the Osa Peninsula one of the most biologically intense locations in the world. Wildlife abounds, monkey, sloth, crocodiles and over 300 species of birds. We also offer scuba diving, snorkeling, fishing and much more!

FLORIDA

Continental Acres Equine Resort 🐴

3000 Marion County Road
P.O. Box 68
Weirsdale, FL 32195
(352)750-5500   (352)753-3105 fax
e-mail: HorseResrt@aol.com
Web: www.continentalacres.com

Season: Year-round   Guest capacity: 25
Airport: Orlando, FL, shuttle service avail.

Vacation or Train with Your Horse in Sunny Florida.
Gorgeous 265 acre equine resort offering the very best in facilities. Accommodations for both you (guest cottages or private villa), and your horse (box stalls and turnout paddocks). Miles of trails, as well as riding and dressage rings, and for the carriage competitor, cones courses and cross country w/hazards. International trainers available to help you. Combined and pleasure driving. Close to all of Central Florida's Attractions. Short and long term accommodations available.

FLORIDA

Grand Cypress Equestrian Center at Grand Cypress Resort 🐴

One Equestrian Drive
Orlando, FL 32836
(800)835-7377 or (407)239-1938
e-mail: resortinfo@grandcypress.com
Web: www.grandcypress.com

Season: Year-round   Airport: Orlando International

Experience a World-Class Riding Vacation.
World-class facilities offer professional instruction in dressage, hunt seat, combined training, jumping and basic western. The first riding facility in the U.S. to be approved by the prestigious British Horse Society and the site of the BHS exams in the U.S. Clinics, seminars, riding academies and special packages offered throughout the year. Bring your own mounts or use the resort's school horses. Quality horses available for sale. Trail rides over 1,500 acres of natural beauty, for all riders, both seasoned and aspiring.

MICHIGAN
Ranch Rudolf ⊤
6841 Brownbridge Road
Traverse City, MI 49686
(616)947-9529

Season: May-November   Guest capacity: 65 lodge, 150 campground   Airport: Traverse City, MI

Way Out West in Michigan.

195 acre resort surrounded by the Marquette State Forest on the Boardman River. There's more to do at Ranch Rudolf...Horseback riding, canoeing, inner-tubing, archery, stocked trout ponds or river fly-fishing, nature trails, hayrides, tennis, volley ball, horseshoes, swimming pool, and playground. Restaurant & lounge; entertainment Saturday nights; bunkhouse, motel units and campgrounds. Children are very much welcome. Family reunions, corporate meetings.

MONTANA
Bear Creek Lodge 🐎
1184 Bear Creek Trail
Victor, MT 59875
(406) 642-3750   (406) 642-6847 fax

e-mail: info@bear-creek-lodge.com
Web: www.bear-creek-lodge.com

Season: March to December   Guest capacity: 16   Airport: Missoula, MT

Take Your Own Horse Along to an Exclusive Luxury Destination.

Bear Creek Lodge is an 8 room, full service, luxury, destination lodge on 115 acres adjacent to the largest wilderness in Montana. There are over 30 trails at the lodge or within a 30 minute drive. We have private fishing access to Bear Creek and the Bitterroot River is only 10 minutes from the lodge. Pamper yourself during your stay in our hot tub, exercise room and sauna. Enjoy fine dining. Relax in the library. Get up a game on our pool table. All inclusive rates. Golf, tennis, and rafting nearby.

OHIO
Heartland
Country Resort ⊤⌐🐎
2994 Township Road 190
Fredericktown, OH 43019
(800-)230-7030 or (419)768-9300
Web: www.bbhost.com/heartland

Season: Year-round   Guest capacity: 40   Airport: Columbus, OH

Hospitality, Adventure and Romance in the Heart of Ohio.

And a riding stable with many registered horses offering walk-trot-canter riding. Recreation and relaxation abound, with riding in arenas or on wooded trails, swim in the heated pool, play pool in the recreation room or cross-country ski over the rolling countryside, compete in a game of basketball, ping pong, or horseshoes, lounge on the deck or screened porch, have a candle lit meal in the 1878 dining room, watch movies in the sitting room, AND unwind in your private Jacuzzi at day's end. Near many state forest trail system trailheads.

Tell the resort that you are glad you found them through the Horse Lovers Vacation Guide

⌐ English Riding   ⊤ Western Riding   🐎 Take Your Own Horse

OHIO
Smoke Rise Ranch Resort 🍸🐴
County Road 92
P.O. Box 253
Murray City, OH 43144
(800)292-1732 or (614)592-4077

Season: Year-round   Airport: Columbus, OH   Guest capacity: 300

Experience the West in the "East".
Your activities will take you riding over hundreds of miles of beautiful wooded trail, allow you to experience a working cattle ranch, learn team penning, rope a calf, run the barrels, drive your carriage horse over smooth roads or just relax. Enjoy our heated swimming pool, hot tub, fishing pond, cabins, campsites with hookups, dining, music and dance in our rustic lodge. Bring your own horse, we provide stalls and corrals. Or rent a horse for a guided ride.

OKLAHOMA
Roman Nose Resort Lodge 🍸🐴
Rt 1
Watonga, OK 73772
(800)654-8240 or (580) 623-7281

Season: Year-round   Guest Capacity: 175

Roman Nose State Park Resort Lodge.
Nestled in a canyon, 80 miles NW of Oklahoma City. 47 inviting guest rooms, two meeting rooms, an activity room, 10 cottages equipped with kitchenettes and full service restaurant. Located in Roman Nose Resort Park. Tennis, golf, fishing, paddleboats, mini-golf, hiking trails, swimming pool (seasonal) and Roman Nose Resort Stables equestrian program.

VERMONT
Mountain Top Inn & Resort 🍸🍸
Mountain Top Road
Chittenden, VT 05737
(800)445-2100   (802)483-2311
(802)483-6373 fax
e-mail: info@mountaintopinn@.com
Web: www.mountaintopinn.com
Season: April to November   Guest Capacity: 135
Airport: Burlington, or Rutland, VT

Elegant Four-Season Country Inn Resort.
This is the home of Vermont Riding Vacations. Spectacular views, relaxing atmosphere and fine dining. Trail ride up to 6 hours per day, or take English or Western lessons in equitation, jumping, dressage or introductory cross country jumping. Walk-trot-canter riding. In addition, enjoy swimming, canoeing, kayaking, fly-fishing, golf & golf school, tennis, claybird shooting, and hiking. Cross-country skiing and sleigh rides in winter. This is a wonderful destination for equestrians with non-rider companions, there are so many activities for all.

RIDING STABLES

Never pass through an area without really getting to see it. The ONLY way to really see the country is from the back of a horse. Seek out the nearest riding stable for an hour, afternoon or an all-day tour of the countryside. Local horses and guides will show you their area.

ILLINOIS
Shenandoah Riding Center 🐴 🐎

2000 Territory Drive
Galena, IL 61036
(815) 777-2373
Season: Year-round

In the Galena Territory, a 6,800 Acres to Trail Ride.
Shenandoah Riding Center is located in the rolling hills of Northwestern Illinois. Our facility features a 40 mile trail system, large indoor and outdoor arenas, tack shop, lounge and 48 clean stalls. We offer a vast array of events and services. Clinics, lessons, overnight boarding, and shows. Close to Eagle Ridge Inn & Resort and several Bed & Breakfasts. Scenery and wildlife are unrivaled. Come ride with us here in the beautiful Galena Territory.

IOWA
Toney's Trail Rides 🐴 🐎

RR 2, Box 27
Lemoni, IA 50140
(515)784-6124

Season: Year-round
Airports: Kansas City, MO or Des Moines, IA

Visit the Midwest.
Take a three day trail ride on a large ranch in Iowa. Lodging, meals, horses and equipment included. Book early for June, July and August. We also have openings for hunters and fishermen. All private land with open ground and lots of timber. Bring your own horse or ride ours.

OHIO
The Bob Evans Farm 🐴

P.O. Box 198, St. Rt. 588
Rio Grande, OH 45674
(800)994-3276

Season: Memorial Day to Labor Day   Location: Near Gallpolis, OH   Guest Capacity: 22

Plan Your Family or Group Outing, "Down on the Farm", Where it All Began.
The scenic countryside on the Farm offers both open meadows and wooded trails. HOURLY RIDES, offered daily, are led by our experienced guides trained to provide an enjoyable and informative ride. Please call for our time schedule. Or opt for our OVERNIGHT TRAILRIDE to enjoy a night of fun under the stars at our remote campsite. Enjoy delicious farm meals prepared over a crackling campfire. Or try our PADDLE & SADDLE combination for a unique canoeing, and overnight riding experience.

OREGON
Black Butte Stables

13892 Hawksbeard Road
P.O. Box 8000
Black Butte Ranch, OR 97759-8000
(541)595-2061
E-mail: blackbuttestables.com
Web: www.oregoncowboy.com

Season: Daily, Memorial Day to Labor Day, weekends year-round
Airport: Redmond or Bend, OR   Guest Capacity: 40 or more by prior arrangement.

View the Cascade Mountains of Central Oregon from Horseback.
Knowledgeable guides lead you through Aspen and Pine groves and across creeks on the 1/2 hour, 1-1/2 hour, 2 hour, half day and all day adventure rides. Try one of our meal rides featuring a hearty western breakfast, or an authentic western barbecue. Tell us what you would like to see and we will put together a ride that will be the highlight of your visit to Central Oregon. Horse boarding is available for those traveling with horses. Pony rides for the young buckaroos, and western riding lessons too.

OREGON
Eagle Crest Equestrian Center

1522 Cline Falls Road
Redmond, OR 97756
(541)504-9799
Web: www.oregoncowboy.com

Season: Daily, Memorial Day to Labor Day, weekends year-round

Take in a View of the Deschutes Aboard a Great Trail Horse.
Weave through Juniper and fragrant sagebrush on an experienced trail horse behind a knowledgable guide on our 1/2 hour, 1 hour, 1-1/2 hour, 2 hour, or half day riding adventures. Spend an afternoon in a horsedrawn wagon or carriage, or take in a horse show at our lighted arena. Gentle ponies are available for young buckaroos as well. We offer stalls and paddocks for horse boarding, and our arena is available for special events. We are located 4 miles west of Redmond on U.S. Highway 126.

OREGON
Running Y Stables

5419 Running Y Road
Klamath Falls, OR 97601
(541)850-5500
Web: www.oregoncowboy.com

Season: Daily, Memorial Day to Labor Day, weekends year-round

Enjoy Southern Oregon's Klamath Lake Area From the Back of a Quarter Horse.
Ride through cattle just as the old cowboys did on our 1/2 hour, 1 hour, 1-1/2 hour, 2 hour, or half day riding adventures. Running Y Stables uses only modern, first rate tack and our wranglers will knock themselves out to give you a great riding experience. We have ponies for the young buckaroos, and horse boarding is available for travelers with horses. We are located 6 miles west of Klamath Falls, Oregon on Highway 140.

 English Riding   Western Riding   Take Your Own Horse

TAKING YOUR OWN HORSE
ON VACATION

When contacting a destination site ask what stabling facilities are like for your horses... picket lines, tie or box stall, private pen or corral.

When you decide to take your own horse along it will take extra planning to locate places to vacation with your horse. You will find many places throughout our directory that allow you to bring private horses. You will find them scattered throughout the categories. Some are simple overnight horse motels, others elaborate full service resorts. To have help in locating overnight accommodations consult our Overnight Stabling section. An agency such as Equine Travellers of America can help you and make reservations for you as you travel.

When contacting a destination ask what stabling facilities are like for private horses...picket lines, tie stall or box, private pen or corral. It is not advisable to turn your horse out with others. The natural pecking order of the horse kingdom will find your horse, the newcomer, at the bottom. If the dominant horse decides to challenge the newcomer your horse might be injured.

A month before you go, take your trailer in to have it checked out. Make sure the brakes are not worn. Are the fluids at proper levels? When trailers sit parked their tires will start to dry rot. This will lead to cracks in the side walls long before the tread starts to wear down. Are the lights properly exhibiting turn signals and brake lights? Check the floor boards for weak spots.

Make sure you have the proper vet papers and shots at least a month before you go. Your vet should have a guide to interstate health requirements. All states require a current EIA test and Certificate of Veterinary Inspection. Some within 3 months of departure. You also need to carry proof of ownership. This could be a registration certificate, bill of sale or brand registration.

One point many people don't consider is making sure their horses are in condition to be able to work on that trip. Get out for some extensive riding before you go so that you won't overdo it and cause serious health problems. If you live at low altitude note that it is very hard on horses to go to high altitudes and immediately be put to hard work climbing mountains. I have seen horses tie up from this practice even though they were in reasonable shape before going. You need to think. If it is hard for you to exercise and breathe it is for your horse too. Know where you are going and what you will encounter before you go.

Take your normal grain along when you travel. Horses do best when they are maintained on the same feed so take along enough to see them through. Many horses refuse to drink water that is different from home. Take some along from home. As much as you can carry. You may be able to wean them over on to new water by adding a little at a time to yours. There is always the possibility that they will happily enjoy what is available. But it is absolutely essential that they not become dehydrated and end up with an impaction.

As you travel down the road it is advisable to stop every 4 or 5 hours to allow the horses to relax. It's good for the driver as well. If possible find a spot where you can take them out and stretch their legs. Don't be in a hurry. Travel at moderate speeds and make slow corners. If you ever played the childhood game of crack the whip you will know how your horse feels at the back of your trailer, when you are cornering fast. Don't chance knocking him off his feet. Drive defensively, look far ahead and anticipate slowing traffic and turns.

Take care and both you and your horse will enjoy that vacation.

Look for these Take Your Own Horse Adventures
Also, see U.S. Trail Systems...page 136 - 146

Alabama – Shady Grove Ranch
Arizona – Flying E Ranch
Arizona – Kay El Bar Ranch
Arizona – Reidhead Outfitters
California – The Homestead
California – Hunewill Guest Ranch
California – Monte Vista Camp
California – Ricochet Ridge Ranch
California – Rock Creek Outfitters
Canada – Black Cat Guest Ranch
Colorado – Brushy Creek Ranch
Colorado – Buffalo Horn Ranch
Colorado – Mountain Meadows Ranch
Florida – Continental Acres Equine Resort
Florida – Grand Cypress Resort
Georgia – Sunburst Stables
Idaho – Kingston 5 Ranch
Illinois – Bear Branch Horse Camp
Illinois – Circle B Ranch
Illinois – Hideout
Illinois – Shenandoah Riding Center
Indiana – Conygar
Iowa – Toney's Trail Rides
Kentucky – Double J Campground
Kentucky – Wranglers Campground
Louisiana – St John Ranch
Michigan – Cedar Lodge
Michigan – Double JJ Resort
Mississippi – Big Sand Campground
Missouri – Golden Hills Campground
Missouri – Wilderness Trail Ride
Montana – Bear Creek Lodge
Montana – D/J Bar Ranch
Montana – Monture Face Outfitters
Montana – Sandcreek Clydesdales
Montana – Sweetgrass Ranch
Montana – TX Ranch
Nevada – Humbolt County Fairgrounds
Nevada – Stonehouse Country Inn
Nevada – Tin Cup Adventures
New Hampshire – Chebacco Ranch
New Hampshire – Horse Haven B&B
New Mexico – Makin' Tracks
New Mexico – Rancho Canon Ancho
New York – Barkeater Inn
New York – Makin' Tracks
New York – Ridin HY Ranch

North Carolina – Burnside B&B
North Dakota – Dahkota Lodge & Trail Rides
Ohio – Heartland Country Resort
Ohio – McNutt Farm II
Ohio – Palmerosa Campgrounds & Cabins
Ohio – Smoke Rise Horseman's Resort
Oklahoma – Indian Mounds Camp
Oklahoma – Roman Nose Campgrounds
Oklahoma – Tickled Pink Ranch
Oregon – Black Butte Stables
Oregon – Eagle Crest Equestrian Center
Oregon – Running Y Stables
Pennsylvania – Artillery Ridge Campgrounds
Pennsylvania – Flying W Ranch
Pennsylvania – Mountain Trail Horse
South Carolina – Mt Carmel B&B
South Dakota – Bunkhouse B&B
South Dakota – Mountain Meadows Resort
South Dakota – Triple R Ranch
South Dakota – Two Bar T Ranch
Tennessee – Charit Creek Lodge
Tennessee – Flintlock Inn & Stables
Tennessee – Gilbertson's Lazy Horse Retreat
Tennessee – Sweet Annie's Bed & Breakfast
Tennessee – Wild Heart Ranch
Texas – Knolle Farm & Ranch
Utah – Ruby's Outlaw Trail Rides
Virginia – Conyers House Inn & Stable
Virginia – Fort Valley Stables
Virginia – Inn at Meander Plantation
Virginia – The Hunting Box
Virginia – Jordan Hollow Farm Inn
Virginia – Penmerryl Farm
Washington – Silver Ridge Ranch
West Virginia – Swift Level
Wyoming – Absaroka Mountain Lodge
Wyoming – Box R Ranch
Wyoming – Pole Creek Ranch
Wyoming – Powder River Experience
Wyoming – Terry Bison Ranch
Wyoming – Triple EEE Ranch
Wyoming – TX Ranch
Nationwide – AQHA Ride Program
Nationwide – Equine Travellers of America
Nationwide – Horseman's Travel Guide
Nationwide – Trail Rider Magazine

Horse Packing Lightly with Your Own Horses

–Excerpt from the U.S.D.A. Forest Service pamphlet – Horse Sense.

PLANNING
Before You Go

Information?

Before you go, contact local land managers for maps, regulations and opportunities for the area, information and rules concerning permits, campfire, party size, grazing, feed, trail conditions and closures, and more. Make alternate plans in case of bad weather.

Know your stock: Which animal leads best? Which ones follow better? Which is the slowest traveler? The slowest animal determines the speed of the pack string. Are they familiar with trails, packing, and with the equipment you plan to use? Get your animals used to highlines, pickets, hobbles and various temporary corrals before you go. Make sure that both yourself and your stock are in shape before you go. It's easier to travel outdoors when both you and your animals are in shape for the trip.

If you plan to pack in bear country, especially grizzly country, make sure you obtain and understand special safety and food storage regulations. Be aware of where bears live, eat, and travel. Food odors can attract hungry or curious bears and other animals too, so it is important to store your food properly. In some areas, this means using bear-proof boxes and panniers.

Supplemental Horse Feed

Don't get caught unprepared when you find your favorite grassy meadow is dry or overgrazed. Take supplemental feed and get your stock used to it at home. Ask local land managers about available grazing and restrictions, so you know how much supplemental feed to bring and where to camp. Many areas permit only certified weed-seed-free feed because some feed contains seeds of noxious weeds and non-native plants. Contact the local Forest Service for sources. Once established, noxious weeds such as spotted knap weed and leafy spurge can spread and destroy grazing for future stock and wildlife. Use nosebags or mangers to feed your stock hay, pellets or grain. They help reduce waste, you don't have to feed stock on the ground, it's easier on the land.

PACKING
The Bare Essentials

Lightweight, compact camp equipment – sleeping bags, tents, camp stoves, cookware, and utensils - help reduce the number of pack animals, allowing you to take what you really need. Try prepackaged meals, dehydrated or freeze-dried food, or repackage food to save space and to reduce weight. Use lightweight, reusable plastic bags instead of glass and cans. For short trips, carry enough water for the area you are in. Or, check into water filtering devices for longer trips. A giardia filter is highly recommended. A shovel, axe and water container are useful for fire safety and keeping camp clean. Use these tools to clear brush and trees that fall across trails when you can do so safely. Take insect repellent and a first aid kit for both yourself and your stock. Make sure you know how to use these before you go.

Camping With Your Horse

Your animals are important. Without them you would have a heavy load to carry. Keep them safe and secure at night.

Highlines in use

Tieing and Tethering

Whether you are camping in the backcountry or in a campground it is important to keep horses safe at night. Most commercial campgrounds have this worked out for you. Many have highline ropes strung up to tie to. Others have corrals or stalls. It is best to find this out before you travel so there are no surprises.

Proper use of tree saver straps to put up your highline

Tree Saver Straps should be at least 2" wide. They are easily made from a recycled seat belt.

Not all areas have horse camps set up. In backcountry National Forest camps and Wilderness areas, keep pack animals at least 200 feet from streams, lake shores, trails, and camping areas. This helps keep water clean, protects the soil and plants, and keeps trails and campsites clear of loose stock.

If you are stringing up your own highline picket ropes, use Tree-Saver Straps. A highline is one of the easiest, lightweight ways to keep your stock in camp. It is easier to put up with a tree-saver strap. The highline prevents stock from trampling roots and chewing bark.

If you must tie stock to a hitching rail or dead pole, tie a four-to-six inch round pole between two trees. Place padding or wooden shims under the lash ropes to protect the bark. Use rope or twine instead of nails or wire. Don't cut standing trees.

Hobbles work for some animals, others can move fast while wearing them. It is easy for them to canter, hobbled. Again, get your stock used to them ahead of time.

How to Use Highlines

1. Choose a durable spot. Hard and rocky ground is best

2. Place tree-savers and rope about 7 feet from the ground.

3. Stretch the line tautly between two trees using adjustable, nylon tree-saver straps.

4. Run the rope between the straps, tie with a quick release knot, and pull tight.

5. Tie horses to highline about 7 feet apart and at least 6 feet from trees.

You could bring an easy-to-move picket pin – such as a metal one, to drive into the ground and tie your horse to. Avoid areas with obstacles so the rope doesn't get hung up. If you walk your animal to the end of the rope before turning it loose, it's less likely to injure itself by running past the end of the rope. Train them not to panic should the rope get around their feet, at home before you travel. Make sure you move your pin and horses frequently throughout the area to reduce trampling and prevent overgrazing of any single area into a recognizable circle.

Picket Stakes

Temporary Fences and Corrals

When you plan to spend several days in one spot, a temporary corral or fence is a good way to keep your stock in camp. If you find permanent corrals at trailheads or designated horse camps, use them! Try some of these temporary fences and corrals, (don't forget to try them out at home and to take them with you).

Plastic snow fences
This fencing is light weight, easy to pack, and comes in colors such as green and black. Some people use a strand of electric fence at the top to prevent stock from escaping.

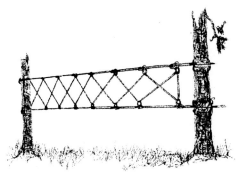

Electric fences
Portable, electric fencing is a convenient temporary corral for stock trained to respect it. It is lightweight, portable, and can run on flashlight batteries. Wildlife sometimes go through electric fences, so be sure to place it away from game trails and any other trails.

Rope Corrals
Rope corrals are relatively easy to rig and move, but they do require extra rope. One method uses two parallel ropes tied with loops of bowlines and threaded with cross ropes for a more secure enclosure.

Packing Tip: What ever way you decide to contain your horses while camping, make sure you train them to accept it before you ride out on the trail.

MAKING CAMP

Keeping It Clean
At last, you've found your spot. Hmm, looks like other people like this place too. Some areas receive lots of visitors, and they don't all follow the "Pack It In, Pack It Out" philosophy. Should you stay here and clean it up, or let the next person take care of it? You've decided to improve your site? Good for you!

Like most people, you enjoy campsite privacy and solitude. Where should you put stock and gear? You can follow the "200 foot guideline", keep stock and gear at least 200 feet from the nearest lakes and streams, meadows, trails, and other camps. In designated Wilderness, this is a requirement which helps keep streams and lakes clean, protects the soil and plantlife, and keeps trails and campsites clear of loose stock. It's helpful to follow it is all areas

Picking a spot
Select an open, well-drained, level spot. In Wilderness areas, you must follow the 200 foot guideline. Rotate stock throughout the area to reduce trampling and prevent overgrazing.

Cleaning Up – Soaps, Detergents, and Waste Materials
For washing chores, use a basin at least 200 feet from water sources. Water plants and fish are extremely sensitive to soap, even biodegradable soap, and can die from it.

To prevent contaminating water sources with stock or human waste, dump it at least 200 feet from water, camp and trails. Use biodegradable, unscented white toilet paper. Bury human waste and toilet paper in a small "cat hole" in the top 6 to 8 inches of soil, or use a latrine for large parties or long stays. Cover you latrine completely.

Campfires
Where fires are allowed, we all enjoy the romance of a campfire. However, campfires sterilize the soil, blacken rocks, and leave long lasting scars on the land. Build them where campfires were previously built. Keep your fires small, attend them while burning and let them burn down to a fine ash, then stir, scatter or pack out ashes according to local practice for that site. Don't cut living trees for firewood, use only deadwood.

These are good alternatives to traditional campfires. Fires built in fire pans are similar to campfires on the ground, but cause less damage. You can also use a cookstove instead of a fire, it's light, convenient, and reduces impacts to the land.

Structures
Rock walls, log benches, lean-tos, and other structures detract from and needlessly impact the natural landscape. If you need temporary structures, bring lightweight tenting equipment with you.

BREAKING CAMP – Pack It In, Pack It Out!"

1. Pack out all refuse, burned cans, unburned campfire debris, and garbage - including food scraps, grease, aluminum foil, and paper.

2. Burn what trash you can. Burying garbage or burning aluminum foil is not an acceptable disposal method and is illegal in some locations.

3. Break up and scatter horse manure and fill in pawed holes.

4 Scatter a covering of needles and cones over the site.

> *The Horseperson's Creed: "When I ride out of the mountains I'll leave only hoofprints, take only photographs... and all the extra garbage I can pack out!"*

TOURS

Tour special scenic areas on trips that emphasis the most important features of the area. The history as well as the natural features. These tour companies will provide you with your mount and guides that know the history and local legends.

ARIZONA /UTAH
Monument Valley 🐎
Trail Rides

P.O. Box 310155
Mexican Hat, UT 84531
(435)739-4285 phone/ fax

Season: Year-round   Guest capacity: 4-25   Airport: Flagstaff, AZ or Farmington, NM

Ride Fine Mustang Horses Through Monument Valley in Utah and Arizona.
The area is well known for the many western movies which have been filmed here. Expert Navajo guides know this gorgeous red rock area well. View the mesas, buttes and slender towering pinnacles. They have a great respect for the land and are happy to share their legends and lore with you. The stable is located within the Navajo Tribal Visitor Park. Explore this magical land on hourly, half-day, all-day and overnight rides that can last up to 7 days. Moonlight rides, sunrise, sunset and daylight tours.

MEXICO
Saddling South
Baja Pack Trips 🐎

P.O. Box 827
Calistoga, CA 94515
(800)398-6200
(707)942-4550 phone/fax

e-mail: tourbaja@iname.com
web: www.tourbaja.com

Season: October-May
Guest Capacity: 3-8
Airport: Loreto, or Baja California Sur, Mexico.   Airport pickup available.

Grab Your Sombrero for an Incredible Journey, into the Heart of the Sierra Giganta.
Saddling South takes you along volcanic ridges, through cactus garden valleys and into the lush palm springs in Baja's spectacular desert mountains. Owner Trudi Angell, with 20 years experience exploring this magnificent peninsula, offers a chance to learn traditions and histories of the remote ranching lifestyle unique to Baja, Mexico. Join us as our local guides share their wisdom and lore along the original missionary trails of the Californias.

When contacting any of the destinations in this directory be sure to tell them that you found them in the Horse Lovers Vacation Guide.

TRAIL RIDING VACATIONS

Hit the trail! Enjoy American, Canadian or worldwide trail systems from horseback. The best way to see the unique trails of an area is to go with a guide, or get a local trail map to ride on your own.

ARIZONA
Reidhead Outfitters 🐴
P.O. Box 596
Alpine, AZ 85920
(520)339-1936

Season: April to October   Airport: Tucson, AZ   Guest Capacity: 10

Ride the Beautiful Wilderness of Alpine, Arizona.
Come experience the White Mountains of Arizona. Enjoy scenic views and plentiful wildlife. See the Aspen, Pine and Fir trees that crowd the horizon. With experienced guides and gentle livestock ride into the wilderness from 6,000 to 9,000 ft altitude. A variety of trails allow for the length of daily rides to be adjusted by the wishes of our clients. 25 years guiding happy guests into this area. This is a very scenic area so bring your camera and lots of film.

CALIFORNIA
Armstrong Woods Pack Station
Box 970
Guerneville, CA 95446
(707)887-2939
Web: www.metro.net/ayers

Season: Year-round   Airport: Santa Rosa or San Francisco, CA

Horseback Adventures Through the Giant Redwoods! Trail Rides and Pack Trips.
Trailrides, overnight camp or cabin, and pack trips through giant redwoods and coastal mountain wilderness, 80 miles north of San Francisco. Nearby Sonoma-Napa wine country, Russian River resort area, and rugged Pacific coast. Family-run outfit specializes in small personalized rides. Excellent AQHA horses for all levels. Instruction. Fresh gourmet meals. Naturalist-guided rides and monthly "women only overnights" also. Inspiring vistas, pristine streams, protected wildlife.

CALIFORNIA
Red's Meadow Pack Station
& Agnew Meadows Pack Station
P.O. Box 395
Mammoth Lakes, CA 93546
(800)292-7758 (760)934-2345 - summer   (760)873-3928 - winter
Web: www.mammothweb.com/redsmeadow

Season: Mid-June to Mid-October   Airport: Reno, NV

The Eastern High Sierra is the "Hidden Treasure" of California.
Trail rides and pack trips into Yosemite National Park and the Ansel Adams / Minaret Wilderness as well as the John Muir Wilderness and Sequoia King National Park. Over 100 lakes and miles of streams available in some of the finest scenery of the High Sierra. Over 40 years of providing quality service. Many interesting loop trips of various duration.

CANADA – Québec
Au Jal A Cheval, Inc. 🐎
82, Rang XII
Auclair, Québec, Canada G0L 1A0   (418)899-6635
    Season: May 15 - October 15   Guest capacity: 10   Airport: Mont-Joli, Québec

The Most Beautiful Vacation on Horseback.
Discover the grandeur of our 150 miles of trails through the lakes, mountains and rivers of the Northern Appalachians in Québec, Canada. Enjoy a different cottage every night and hearty meals served by our attentive staff. A thrilling ride in the heart of nature for everyone who loves horses.

CANADA – Alberta
Holiday on horseback 🐎
Box 2280
Banff, AB, T0L 0C0 CANADA
(800)661-8352 or (403)762-4551
e-mail: warner@horseback.com
Season: May-October   Guest capacity: 4-20   Airport: Calgary, AB

The Ultimate Trail Riding Adventures in Banff National Park.
Ride the Cascade Valley Range for a mountain wilderness experience you will never forget, 3 to 6 days. Your guides, saddle horses, cooks, packers, delicious meals and back-country tenting accommodations included. Prices begin around $105 U.S. per day. Both camps and moving pack trips available. Or if you wish the joy of riding through the wilderness without camping, enjoy nature's best at Sundance and Halfway Lodges from overnight to 6 days. Nature study packages.

CANADA – Québec
Ranch Massif du Sud, Inc. 🐎🐎
149 Rte, Massif du Sud
St Philémon, Québec, Canada G0R 4A0
(418) 469-2900
Season: Year-round   Guest capacity: 17   Airport: Québec City

Live the Gold Rush. Live a True Adventure on Horseback.
Cross the Appalachian Mountains with their spectacular views and the valleys through Maple forest and along rivers for gold panning and fishing. Marvel at the abundant wildlife. There are a variety of rides from 1 to 10 days in length. Meals and lodging at the ranch or rustic cabins. Hear the gold story legend of this country retold around a blazing campfire. Also horseback fishing and hunting. Special activities for groups. Discover winter riding, horse and dog sleigh rides, snow mobile, and ski.

COLORADO
Weminuche Wilderness Adventures 🐎
17754 County Road 501
Bayfield, CO 81122
(970)884-2555 summer   (602)471-0065 winter
Season: June - September   Guest capacity: 4-8.   Airport: Durango, CO

The Weminuche on Horseback – Truly the Experience of a Lifetime!
Return to the joys and exhilarations of a lost way of life on a pack trip into the wilderness area of the San Juan Mountains. On this exciting adventure we reach deep into majestic mountain back country, comfortably mounted on well-trained horses, being outdoors for every part of every day where land and nature are still peaceful and free.

ILLINOIS
Bear Branch Horse Camp 🐎 🐴
PO Box 40, HWY 145
Eddyville, IL 62928
(616)672-4249   (618)672-4739 fax
e-mail: manders@shawnee.link.com

Season open: Year-round   Airport: Nashville, KY
Guest capacity: 4 cabins, 80 campsites w/hookups, 40 acres of primitive camping

Bear Branch Horse Camp, Outfitter, Log Cabin Restaurant and the Ultimate Trail Ride.
Overlooking Lusk Creek Canyon, one of the most scenic areas in the 275,000 acre Shawnee National Forest. Ride our lush forest trails, ford rocky creeks, travel down rock canyons, circle & climb high bluffs under waterfalls into large caves, you'll see why this is the home of the Ultimate Trail Ride. Featuring a Rustic Log Cabin Restaurant, tack shop, general store, a barn with 40 bedded horse stalls. Heated and air conditioned shower house with laundry facilities, dump station, a 2 acre pond for swimming and fishing, and cabins for rent as well as trail horses. Trail Guide in camp at all times.

GEORGIA
Sunburst Stables 🐎 🐴
3181 State Hwy 255
Clarkesville, GA 30523
(706)947-7433
Season: Year-round   Guest capacity: 15   Airport: Atlanta, GA

Ride the Northern Blue Ridge Mountains Near Clarkesville, Georgia.
Come ride through miles of beautiful mountain scenery on your horses or ours! We offer guided trail rides into the National Forest of 1 hour up to overnight. Camping or lodging adventures. All levels of riding experience are welcome. A cross-country course is available for those interested in jumping. Several types of lodging offered: 16 person bunkhouse, 4 person cabins with hot tubs or primitive camping.

HAWAII
King's Trail Rides O'Kona 🐎
P.O. Box 1366
Kealakehua, HI 96750-1366   (808) 323-2388
e-mail: bones@interpac.net   Web: www.interpac.net/~hit/ktr.html
Season: Year-round   Guest capacity: 4 - 6   Airport: Kailua - Kona, HI

Trail Ride and Snorkel in Paradise!
Ride along the old "Kings Trail" to an ancient Hawaiian village at Kealakekua Bay. Explore where Capt. Cook landed and check out the monument that has been erected in his honor. We also provide masks and snorkels so you can enjoy some of the best snorkeling on the island.

KENTUCKY
Wrangler's Campground 🐎
100 Van Morgan Drive
Golden Pond, KY 42211
(800)LBL-7077   (502)924-2087 fax   Web: www.lbl.org
Season: Year-round   Airport: Nashville, TN

Wranglers Campground at Land Between the Lakes, National Recreation Area.
Ride along 75 miles of horse trails and wagon roads. Our campground features camping shelters, electric sites, bath houses, stalls and stables, an outpost supply center, tack and farrier service.

MEXICO
Saddling South
Baja Pack Trips
P.O. Box 827
Calistoga, CA 94515
(800)398-6200
(707)942-4550 phone/fax
e-mail: tourbaja@iname.com
web: www.tourbaja.com
Season: October-May
Guest capacity: 3-8
Airport: Loreto, or Baja California Sur, Mexico.   Airport pickup available.

Grab Your Sombrero for an Incredible Journey, into the Heart of the Sierra Giganta.
Saddling South takes you along volcanic ridges, through cactus garden valleys and into the lush palm springs in Baja's spectacular desert mountains. Owner Trudi Angell, with 20 years experience exploring this magnificent peninsula, offers a chance to learn traditions and histories of the remote ranching lifestyle unique to Baja, Mexico. Join us as our local guides share their wisdom and lore along the original missionary trails of the Californias.

MONTANA
WTR Outfitters, Inc.
520 Cooper Lake Rd
Ovando, MT 59854
(800)WTR-5666 or (406) 793-5666
Season: June-Dec.   Guest capacity: 6 - 20
Airport: Missoula, MT

**Great Trail Riding At It's Best
With The Best Since 1940!**
High adventure on horseback with over 1200 miles of trails to explore. View the Chinese Wall, ice caves or historic Danaher Valley. Ride well trained horses over mountain passes and into the beautiful valleys of the Bob Marshall Wilderness complex. Enjoy campfire tales of present and past, experience nature at it's finest. Learn new skills while enjoying a comfortable camp and excellent meals.

NEVADA
Tin Cup Adventures Υ
220 Wayne Road
Carson City, NV 89704
(702)849-0570
e-mail: mdtristram@webtv.net
Web: www.alternatesolutions.com/tincup
Season: Year-round   Guest capacity: 8   Airport: Reno, NV

Spend a Day or a Week on Horseback, Sight Wildlife and Wild Horses.
Ride in beautiful country from high desert to High Sierra. Northwestern Nevada is our range and we ride a big piece of it. Along the way we check on the wildlife and wild horses and camp in the prettiest places you can imagine. Great for families, experienced riders or first-time riders. A real riding adventure. Come now while the land is pristine or stand in line later.

NATIONWIDE
The Trail Rider Magazine 🐴
147 Sun Ridge Road
Alexandria, LA 71302
(800)448-1154 or (318)448-1659
(318)487-8608 fax

The TRAIL RIDER Magazine Is Devoted To Trail Riding.
The Trail Riders Information Source! We have over 800 rides listed throughout the United States. Trail rides, vacations on horseback and wagon trains. We have articles concerning ride information, horse care, a veterinarian column, tips for the new horseman, endurance riding columns and much more! The TRAIL RIDER Magazine is published bi-monthly.

NEW MEXICO
Rancho Cañón Ancho 🐎 🐴
P.O. Box 303
Wagon Mound, NM 87752
(505)666-2004
Season: May – October
Guest capacity: 16   Airport: Albuquerque, NM

Ride into the Old Wild West on Your Own Horse or One of Ours!
Camp under star filled skies in a Wall Tent, on our remote family owned & operated cattle ranch. Fish, float or swim the Mora River. Learn how to handle the herd, or just relax around the cracklin' campfire & listen to the Coyotes sing. Chuckwagon meals beef eaters or Vegans will enjoy. Hot showers, wildlife safaris, nature hikes, hayrides, historical trips along the Santa Fe Trail. Trailriders, endurance riders, family vacationers... enjoy warm, western hospitality. Rates & packages flexible.

NEW YORK
The Bark Eater Inn 🐎 🐴
Alstead Hill Rd.
P.O. Box 139
Keene, NY 12942
(518)576-2221   (518)576-2171 fax
E-mail: barkeater@trenet.com
Web: www.tvenet.com/barkeater.com
Season: Year-round   Guest capacity: 30
Airport: Albany, NY or Burlington, VT, pickup available

Beginner or Old Hand...
this 19th century inn set in a quiet Adirondack valley is for you. Trails and country roads beckon. Full size ring, instruction in English, western, and polo available. The Inn, carriage house and log cottage are filled with antiques. Full country breakfast included; gourmet dining by reservation. Olympic sites and cultural attractions are 15 minutes away in Lake Placid. Families welcome. Trailering encouraged. A true country inn, livery and stable. Cross-country ski center.

Trail riding tip: At rest stops - even short ones - tie your stock off the trail. This is courteous to other trail users and helps reduce wear and tear on the trail. Don't let your horses chew on tree bark. If you have a horse prone to do this take and extra lead rope and cross tie them between trees. Before you move on scatter the manure.

NEW YORK
Makin' Tracks, LLC
Rd 1, Box 130C
Carthage, NY 13619
(315) 346-1049 (315) 376-4539 fax
e-mail: mary@huntcamp.com
Season Spring to Fall Guest capacity: 8

Licensed NYS Guides Lead You on Unique Trips Through the Western Adirondacks.
Upon your own horse, experience scenic views of pristine wilderness and enjoy sighting various
wildlife and plants. Be it a day ride or an extended stay, relax around a campfire while we prepare
some tasty local favorites. Savor the clean air and chuckle while listening to the folklore of the region.
Rides are tailored to the experience level of both horse and rider.

NORTH DAKOTA
Dahkotah Lodge & Trail Rides
P.O. Box 465
Medora, ND 58645   (701)623-4897
Season: April 1 to October 15   Guest capacity: 25   Airport: Bismarck, ND

Trail Ride, Work Cattle, Pack Trips, Your Horse or Ours.
Ride some of the most spectacular country, work cattle on our fourth generation, 13,000 acre ranch.
Sleep on comfortable beds in log cabins, camp out in remote campsites or stay in your own RV. Ride
our gentle, well trained horses, or bring your own. Plenty of wildlife, bighorn sheep, eagles, wild
turkey, pheasant, antelope, deer, so bring your camera. Join a pack trip, from overnight to four days.

OHIO
Palmerosa
Horse Camp
19217 Keifel Road
Laurelville, OH 43135
(614)385-3799
Season: Year-round   Airport: Columbus, OH

**Camp Here or Rent Our Bunkhouses or Cabins and Ride
Your Horse Through the Breathtaking Hocking Hills.**
Ride in caves and box canyons, see waterfalls and large rock formations. Our scenic tall hills and deep forests will convince you that southern Ohio is not just flat farmland! Write for literature on our annual organized rides (see "Annual Trail Rides" for dates). Open year-round. Electric and non-electric hookups, well shaded campsites, showers, bunkhouses and cabins.

PENNSYLVANIA
Artillery Ridge Campgrounds
& the National Riding Stable
610 Taneytown Road
Gettysburg, PA 17325
(717)334-1288
Season: April 1-November 30   Airport: Harrisburg, PA

Ride the Historic Gettysburg Battlefield.
Feel a sense of history as you ride the battlefield as our forefathers did. Bring your own horses, we have box stalls and corrals to stable them. Or ride one of ours on a guided ride across the battle fields. Try our 2 hour ride accompanied by a Licensed Battlefield Guide that includes the Pickett's Charge area. We have 112 electric and water sites and acres of non-hookup sites. Your camping includes FREE hot showers, swimming pool, stocked fishing and much more.

PENNSYLVANIA
Mountain Trail
Horse Center, Inc.
RD 2, Box 53G
Wellsboro, PA 16901
(717) 376-5561
Web: www2.epix.net/~mthc

Season: Year-round   Guest capacity: 15   Airport: Corning-Elmira, NY or Williamsport, PA

The Most Fun You can Have On Horseback East of the Mississippi!
Ride in Pennsylvania's Grand Canyon country, through vast forests...explore old logging roads, climb mountains...descend into valleys and ford rushing streams... be invigorated by a gallop. Adventurous rides go where motor vehicles can't go...through country you didn't know still existed. Overnight camping rides in unspoiled areas; also day trips, winter ride and ski, and covered wagon rides.

Hints for Smooth Trails
Please stay on the trails. Cutting across switchbacks tramples plants and creates parallel paths which erode severely. Although it's tricky, keep your stock from skirting shallow puddles, small rocks, and bushes. This helps prevent the creation of wide, deteriorating trails.

PENNSYLVANIA
Triple "W" Riding Stable and Double "W" Ranch B&B 🐴

RR 2, Box 1543
Honesdale, PA 18431-9643
(800)540-2620 or (717)226-2620
Season: Year-round   Guest capacity: 20-25   Airport: Scranton, PA

You Won't Find "Follow the Leader" Riding Here in the Poconos!
Triple W's 183 acre secluded mountain top setting, situated high in the lake region of the Poconos. Spectacular scenery, trails past lakes, streams, waterfalls, thru meadows and country roads. Explore trails for beginner to the experienced rider. Over 50 horses. Free instruction. Rides from 1 hour to all day. Horse camping trips, hayrides, pony rides, group trips and outings. Murder Mysteries, winter riding and sleigh rides with jingle bells. Cozy B&B with large dining room, ski lounge, fireplace game room. **Specials, events, workshops and customized outings for your group.**

SOUTH DAKOTA
Mountain Meadow Resort 🐴 🚐

11321 Gillette Prairie Road
Hill City, SD 57745-6526
(605)574-2636 (605)574-4891 fax

Season: May 15-September 30   Airport: Rapid City, SD
Guest capacity: 4 cabins, (5 people each); 25 campsites, (25 families)

The Horseman's Resort!
Explore the Black Hills from the Mountain Meadow Resort located at Deerfield Lake. You will find excellent facilities for yourself and your horses. Stay in the housekeeping cabins or campground which has electrical sites and full hookups, fire pits, water and a bathhouse. Various size corrals house horses. The trail system is well mapped, no guiding necessary. Trails from 4-15 miles long with points of interest along each trail. Close to Mt. Rushmore, Crazy Horse and Custer State Park.

SOUTH DAKOTA
Two Bar T Ranch 🐴 🚐

HCR 30, Box 13
Spearfish, SD 57783
(605)578-2438
e-mail: hoodentp@dtgnet.com
Season: Year-round   Guest capacity: 6   Airport: Spearfish or Rapid City

Bring Your Horse and Ride the Ranch and the National Forest.
The Two Bar T is a working cattle ranch located on the northern edge of the beautiful Black Hills of South Dakota. The newly remodeled homestead log cabin sleeps up to 3 couples and has all the modern amenities. The cabin is nicely decorated with period furnishing to give it a real Old West feeling. The historic 1880's barn has 4 new stalls and a large corral. Between the ranch, the Hills, and the surrounding communities, there is a lot to do and see. Reservations and deposit required.

Hints for Smooth Trails
Use your "horse sense!" It's easy to overlook, but your own or your animals' lives could be at risk in rough country. Let your stock pick their way through boggy places, slide zones, on slick and steep trails, and through deep water and snow. Get off and lead them through treacherous stretches where you are unsure.

TENNESSEE
Charit Creek Lodge ♄ 🐄

Lodge located within Big Southfork
National River and Recreation Area
Reservation office:
250 Apple Valley Road
Sevierville, TN 37862
(423) 429-5704

Season: Year round   Guest capacity: 40   Airport: Knoxville, TN

Charit Creek Lodge Accessible ONLY by Horse or Hiking.
Charit Creek Lodge is a backcountry riding and hiking lodge located deep in the 125,000 acre, Big South Fork National River and Recreation Area. It is accessible only on foot or horseback. The area offers over 150 miles of maintained horse trails. Rustic but very comfortable accommodations. "Family Style" meals are included with overnight stay. Reservations required. Horse stabling available. *An authorized National Park Service concession.*

TENNESSEE
Flintlock Farm ♄ 🐄

790 G'Fellers Road
Chuckey, TN 37641
(423) 257-2489   (423) 257-5547 fax
e-mail: flintloc@aol.com

Season: Year-round   Guest capacity: 6
Airport: Tri-Cities   Airport pickup available

Challenging Riding Adventures in the Land of the First Pioneers.
Come ride with us on beautiful Blue Ridge mountain and valley trails. Create your own package combining unlimited riding with fishing, rafting, canoeing, hiking, and hot-air ballooning. Spectacular mountain views from our lovingly restored and furnished 200 year old log farmhouse. We welcome small groups of experienced riders with warm Southern hospitality, personal attention, cozy accommodations, and great country cooking!

UTAH
All 'Round Ranch ♄

P.O. Box 153 HL
Jensen, UT 84035
(800)603-8069 or (435) 789-7626
e-mail: allaround@easilink.com
Web: www.allroundranch.com

Season: May - November
Guest capacity: 12
Airport: Vernal, UT

Learn Cowboy Horsemanship on Quality Quarter Horses.
Four and six-day adventures scheduled summer through fall. Emphasis on active learning and full participation. Ride rugged rangeland in Utah and Colorado, camp at working cow camps, wrangle cattle. Horsemanship skills taught to all levels of riders, novice to experienced. Over 25 years in adventure-based education. Group size is limited; minimum age of 16 (12 on a family adventure). Featured on the front cover of the Horse Lovers Vacation Guide.

WAGON TRAINS

MONTANA
Sandcreek Clydesdales
Ranch Vacations & Wagon Trains ▼ 🐴
Box 330
Jordan, MT 59337
(406)557-2865 (406)557-2001 fax
e-mail: bev@midrivers.com
Web: www.garfieldcounty.com/wadbev/sandy.html
Season: April 1 to September 30 Airport: Billings, MT

Ranch Vacations To Fit Your Dreams.
Enjoy ranch activities while lodging in a modernized homestead era home. Our annual Wagon Train featuring the Sandcreek Clydesdales is held the last weekend of September. Local neighbors add atmosphere to 3 days of traveling by wagon or riding horseback and 2 evenings of socializing including dining, dancing and camping on the prairie.

WYOMING
Wagons West
Box 1156 R
Afton, WY 83110   ▼
(800)447-4711 or (307)886-9693
(307)886-5284-fax
Season: June-August
Airport: Jackson Hole, WY
Guest Capacity: Average 35

Wagons West Invites You...
To be a part of a Western American replica of a Pioneer Covered Wagon Train in Jackson Hole next to the Tetons. Frequent rest stops and a lunch break provide time to enjoy the natural beauty of the passing scenery • 2-4-6 day treks • Chuckwagon meals • Campfire entertainment nightly • Gentle riding horses • A great Family Vacation for anyone of any age. Call or write for information on our wagon train adventures.

Sunburst Stables
Come ride miles of
beautiful mountain trails with us
on your horse or ours.
Camping and lodging adventures
in the mountains of Georgia.
1-800-806-1953

WILDLIFE OBSERVATION

CALIFORNIA
Wild Horse Sanctuary 🏇
P.O. Drawer 30
Shingletown, CA 96088-0030
(916) 474-5880
Season: April-October

**Visit the Wild Horse Sanctuary to Ride and Experience
the Excitement of Wild Herds Running Free!**
This government-authorized sanctuary for horses provides a permanent home for unwanted wild horses and burros that would otherwise be destroyed. Become a "Friend of the Sanctuary" with a $50 donation, or donate a monthly fee to provide for "your own horse".

UTAH
Hondoo Rivers & Trails 🏇
P.O. Box 98 c/o Lyn
Torrey, UT 84775
(800) 648-8768 reservations
Season: May-October   Airport: Grand Junction, CO or Salt Lake, UT   Guest Capacity: 15

Marvel at the Petroglyphs, Indian Ruins and Colorful Rock Formations.
Explore the red rock canyon country of Capitol Reef National Park. Join a wildlife photo hunt - buffalo, wild horses, elk, or desert bighorn sheep. Good Quarter horses, camping gear, well prepared meals in back country camps on the edge of the wilderness.

Vacationing on the Working Ranch

To be able to step into someone else's shoes, is a rare opportunity. A guest can come from the city one day and try out being a cowboy the next.

" Why would I want to pay someone to do their work? " I am often asked this question by people first contemplating the "Working Ranch Vacation".

To be able to step into someone else's shoes, is a rare opportunity. A guest can come from the city one day and try out being a cowboy the next. And come they do. From all professions, I've met highly paid presidents of large corporations, and aeronautical engineers out there getting dusty and dirty working right along with truck drivers, perfume salesmen, or computer programers. A true working ranch is a great vacation for all ages. The best vacation allows you to do something totally different. The cowboy lifestyle is it. And you get to enjoy a good working cow horse at the same time. You don't really have to do a lot of work. If you would rather just ride along and take pictures you can. You do as much as you feel confident in doing.

There is no way you can become totally proficient at being a cowboy from one ranch week. You go out and try the best you can. Laugh a lot and feel like a kid playing cowboy again. Real western Cowboys really do start riding before they can walk. This amazed me. Visiting Schively Ranch in Montana one year on the occasion of their grand daughter's third birthday, I found out how young they do start. A guest that came often brought her a saddle as a present. Her delight was evident. "Gonna go ride Buck", she said. She wasn't very big, dragging the saddle toward the door she was determined. Her grandpa took the saddle from her and carried it out to the barn. He set it down, and went to rope Buck in the corral. She went straight for the tack room and climbed up several bales of hay to get Buck's bridle. It caught on a high hook but her determination was high. After a couple of tugs down it came, and she ran off to the corral with it. We heard the creak of the corral gate as her Grandfather brought the horse around. We all had expected a pony or small horse. Instead Buck was a large animal. He hoisted the tiny saddle up on Buck's back and needed two girths to make it around Buck's barrel. No sooner had he tightened it than this little girl, whose head didn't even come up to the stirrup was boosted up. She went riding with us that day. No one led her like a city youngster, she hung on and made Buck go the way she wanted.

When contacting a working ranch ask about their herd. The real rancher will tell you with pride about his stock. Before you know it your mind will be thinking of things you have never thought of before, breeding bulls, roping, breaking colts, working horses, calf production, market prices...

Go enjoy yourself, become a cowboy for a week – Be a Kid Again!

WORKING RANCHES

ARIZONA
The Horseshoe Ranch on Bloody Basin Road 🐎🤠

HCR 34, Box 5005
Mayer, AZ 86333
(520)632-8813
e-mail: hranch@primenet.com
Season: September - June
Airport: Phoenix, AZ Guest capacity: 12

Experienced Riders, Become part of the Team That Rides For the Horseshoe Brand.
Experienced riders come to do what they have never done before – work cattle from the saddle of a cattle-savvy ranch horse. Riders find doing real cowboy work the "Ultimate High". 70,000 acres of mesas, canyons and mountains in snow-free Arizona. Saddle up and do what needs to be done that day, sorting, searching for strays, gathering, driving, roping, riding fence, branding and doctoring. Then shower off the trail dust in your own private ranch house room and enjoy a hearty ranch meal.

CALIFORNIA
Hunewill Guest Ranch 🐎🤠

P.O. Box 368 HL
Bridgeport, CA 93517
(760)932-7710   (760)932-7933 fax
Web: www.hunewillranch.com
Season: May - Late September   Guest capacity: 45   Airport: Reno, NV

Hunewill Ranch – Family Owned & Operated Working Cattle Ranch Since 1861. You won't want to go home.!
Horseback riding is our specialty. 130 horses, one just right for you. Children's riding program, breathtaking mountain scenery. Hay rides, dancing, cattle work, Fall Color Ride, 5 day Cattle Drive and more. **Free color brochure.**

COLORADO
Brush Canyon Ranch, CRC Inc. 🐎

8760 Old San Isabel Road
Rye, CO 81069
(719)489-2266

Season: May-October   Guest capacity: 6-8   Airport: Pueblo or Colorado Springs, CO

Ranching Like It Used To Be!
Experience ordinary ranch life on the Christenson Ranch in Colorado's beautiful Greenhorn Mountains. This small, family run outfit is one of the few such operations that remain of what once was the backbone of ranching in America. This third generation ranch family offers you unlimited riding and cattle work on good working cow horses, outstanding scenery, old fashioned western hospitality, delicious home cooked meals and cozy, comfortable accommodations.

COLORADO
Buffalo Horn Ranch 🐎
13825 County Rd. 7
Meeker, CO 81641
(970) 878-5450
Website: http://buffalohornranch.com
Season: May - August
Guest capacity: 30
Airport: Grand Junction, CO

Help Herd Cattle on Our 16,000+ Acre Working Cattle Ranch
in spectacular northwest Colorado. Novices to old hands will have fun helping our cowboys work and doctor the cattle as they change pastures. You'll enjoy lunch on the trail or return to our spacious new lodge for gourmet buffet meals. Relax in the evening around a bonfire or enjoy a game of pool or big screen TV and other amenities of the lodge. Enjoy great scenery, friendly folks, fine food, and outdoor fun at its finest! Please call or write for additional information.

COLORADO
Lost Valley Ranch 🐎🤠
29555 Goose Creek Road, Box HL
Sedalia, CO 80135
(303) 647-2311
lostranch@aol.com
www.ranchweb.com/lost

Season: March 1-December 1   Airport: Colorado Springs, CO   Guest capacity: 90

Discover Our Year 'Round Authentic Working Cattle/Horse Ranch.
Just 80 miles from Denver & Colorado Springs. Blaze new trails while exploring 40,000 acres of the Rocky Mountains. Year 'round riding, cattle roundups, special horsemanship weeks, weekly rodeos and Orvis fishing schools. AAA rated "4 Diamonds". Cabin-suites with fireplace. Weekly all-inclusive adult rates: $1,495 (summer); $700-$1050 (fall-spring).

COLORADO
Roubideau Western Adventures 🐎
3680 Cedar Rd.
Delta, CO 81416
(888)878-9378

Season: Branding: April through May
Cattle Drives and Chuckwagon trips: May to Mid-June
Cowcamps: June - November
Web: www.dci-press.com/roubideau/index.html
Guest capacity: 6 per ranch   Airport: Montrose or Grand Junction, CO, pickup available

RIDE THE RANGE in the Mountains of Western Colorado.
Step back in time and enjoy the simple pleasures of life with real cowboys and cowgirls, as you roundup and trail cattle, check fence, or pack salt in the Uncompahgre National Forest. Experience fresh air, beautiful scenery, wildlife, cow camp cabins, learning and living the "Cowboy Life". Offering personalized true ranch vacations. Each day is a new adventure!

IDAHO
Granite Creek Guest Ranch & Cattle Ranch 🐎

P.O. Box 340
Ririe, ID 83443
(208)538-7140 or (208)525-1104

Season: June-September
Airport: Idaho Falls, ID or Jackson, WY
Guest capacity: 8+

**More Than a Guest Ranch –
Join us for a Family-Oriented,
Authentic Western Vacation.**

Stay in rustic cabins with showers on a scenic mountain working cattle ranch. Stay a day, or a week, or try our 3-day special. Activities for the experienced or novice riders and youngsters too. Trail rides, cattle drives, Snake River float trips and the best fishing in the world. Listen to the call of the coyote, wildlife is abundant. Moose, elk, and deer are often seen. Just 120 miles south of Yellowstone Park and 50 miles west of Jackson Hole. Brochure available.

MONTANA
Blacktail Ranch 🐎

4440 South Fork Trail
Wolf Creek, MT 59648
(406)235-4330

Guest capacity: 30
Airport: Great Falls, MT, pickup available

Spectacular Mountain Working Ranch.
Family owned and operated for over 100 years. We have it all! Unlimited riding on a great string of Paint horses in some of Montana's most beautiful mountains. Over-

night trail rides across the Continental Divide - cattle drives all season - abundant wildlife and wild flowers - hiking trails - 8 miles of private trout stream - day trips on the Missouri River and numerous Native American sites. We also boast newly renovated cabins exceptional home cooking, hot tub and sauna. Western hospitality on a real Montana ranch.

MONTANA
Lazy EL Ranch 🐎

P.O. Box 90
Roscoe, MT 59071
(406)328-6830   (406) 328-6857 fax
e-mail: jchilds@mcn.net

Season: May 15 to September 15
Guest capacity: 15   Airport: Billings, MT

Genuine Ranch Vacation Is Ideal For Families.
Our ranch is 4th generation, family owned and operated, we take one family or party at a time. Come sleep in an historic log lodge built in 1907. Eat in the cookhouse with crew and the owners. Help move and doctor cattle, build fence, clean ditches, or hike, swim, fish and hunt on 15,000 acres in the foothills of the Beartooth Mountains just over the mountains from Yellowstone National Park.

MONTANA/WYOMING
Schively Ranch 🐴🤠

1062 Rd 15, Attn: LJ
Lovell, WY 82431
(307)548-6688

Season: April-November
Guest capacity: 17
Airport: Billings, MT, airport pickup

Genuine Working Cattle Ranch!
This is the real thing. Cattle ranching has

been a way of life for the Bassett family for generations. Visit their ranch and help them work cattle. Ride the range over thousands of acres. Drive, brand, ear tag, cut, rope, trail, wean, roundup, doctor, all activities geared to the needs of the cattle at the time of your visit. Do what the hands do, live their lifestyle. Ride a string of good working Quarter horses. Lodging in cabins on the ranch or tents when working cattle at the far reaches of the range. Hearty ranch meals served family style. Video available,

MONTANA
Sweet Grass Ranch 🐴🐎

HC 87 Box 2161
Big Timber, MT 59011
(406)537-4477 phone/fax
e-mail: sweetgrass@mcn.net
Web: www.sweetgrassranch.com
Season: June 8 to September 8
Guest capacity: 20
Airport: Billings, MT pickup available

Sweet Grass Ranch is a
Working Cattle Ranch...

offering guests the opportunity to ride countless miles of mountain trails and open, rolling country on good horses, and join the family working and moving cattle. Get hands-on experience with horses of all ages, from colts to grown horses, learning to think like they do. Unlimited riding, walk-trot-lope. Family style meals, no TV, no social organization. A real western ranch.

MONTANA/WYOMING
TX Ranch 🐴🐎

P.O. Box 501
Lovell, WY 82431
(307)548-6751

Season: April to October
Guest capacity: 18
Airport: Billings, MT

Live the Life of the Cowboy, Riding
Where Wild Horses Still Run Free.
The TX Ranch covers 30,000 acres from the
rim of the Big Horn Canyon to the Pryor

Mountains on the Montana - Wyoming border. Your involvement with us working cattle makes this an unforgettable vacation! We ride long hours – trailing a herd, roping, branding – whatever needs to be done. Home-cooked meals, tent camping and evenings around the campfire. Visit the Tillett family on this Old-Fashioned working guest cattle ranch, (no frills), and live the real west!

NEW MEXICO
N Bar Ranch 🐴 🐎
P.O. Box 409
Reserve, NM 87830
(800)616-0434 or (505)533-6253

Season: May to October
Guest capacity: 16
Airport: Albuquerque, NM

Have You Ever Thought You Were Born 100 Years Too Late?
Dreams come alive and adventure reigns at the N Bar Ranch. Whether you choose to take part in an authentic 1890's round up and cattle drive, or become an outlaw for a week trying to elude a persistent posse, the past is anything but forgotten here at the N Bar. Maybe you'd opt for a pack trip through the extraordinary beauty of the world's oldest wilderness, or simply choose to relax on your cabin porch knowing you can ride for miles in any direction, anytime you wish. Whatever your fancy, we want to offer you the richest, most unforgettable vacation of your life.

NEW MEXICO
Rancho Cañón Ancho 🐴 🐎
P.O. Box 303
Wagon Mound, NM 87752
(505)666-2004

Season: May – October   Guest capacity: 16   Airport: Albuquerque, NM

Ride into the Old Wild West on Your Own Horse or One of Ours!
Camp under star filled skies in a Wall Tent, on our remote family owned & operated cattle ranch. Fish, float or swim the Mora River. Learn how to handle the herd, or just relax around the cracklin' campfire & listen to the Coyotes sing. Chuckwagon meals beef eaters or Vegans will enjoy. Hot showers, wildlife safaris, nature hikes, hayrides, historical trips along the Santa Fe Trail. Trailriders, endurance riders, family vacationers... enjoy warm, western hospitality. Rates & packages flexible... it's your vacation! You plan it.

SOUTH DAKOTA
Bunkhouse Bed & Breakfast 🐴 🐎
14630 Lower Spring Creek Road
Hermosa, SD 57744
(605)342-5462 or (888)756-5462

Season: May 1-December 31
Guest capacity: 8-10
Airport: Rapid City, SD

Working Ranch Bed and Breakfast with Facilities for Your Horse and Limited Camping.
Load up your favorite horse and hang your hat at our working ranch B&B. Ride in the land where buffalo, deer, antelope and elk roam free. Where cowboys and Indians still make their living off the land. Follow well marked trails, or set off on your own in Custer State Park, Badlands National Park, or on our ranch. Drift off to peaceful sleep listening to the creek and coyotes, awaken to the smell of fresh coffee and be welcomed to our sumptuous "all you can eat" breakfast. Trail maps and guided rides available. Couples, singles, families or small groups welcome.

SOUTH DAKOTA
Two Bar T Ranch 🐎

HCR 30, Box 13
Spearfish, SD 57783
(605)578-2438

Season: Year-round   Guest capacity: 6   Airport: Rapid City, SD

Bring Your Own Horse to Ride the Ranch and Black Hills Trails.
Come vacation in our newly restored fully furnished log cabin located on a working cattle ranch. The ranch sits on the northern edge of the beautiful Black Hills in Western South Dakota. Our cabin sleeps up to 3 couples. Come alone or bring your friends. Comfortable lodging, plenty of riding and lots to do. We are only 8 miles from historic Deadwood, the wild west town that offers gambling, skiing, and snowmobiling. We have large corrals and 4 indoor stalls for your horses.

WYOMING
The Hideout 🐎

3208 Beaver Creek Road
Greybull, WY 82426
(800)FLITNER (354-8637)

Season: June to September   Airport: Cody, WY

Ranch Resort, Cowboy Adventures
A working cattle ranch, founded in 1906, is located in the beautiful rolling foothills of the majestic Big Horn Mountains of Wyoming. Today it offers the opportunity for guests to experience traditional ranch life as well as other outdoor activities, while enjoying upscale rustic western accommodations.

WYOMING
Lozier's
Box "R" Ranch 🐎

Box 100 - HLVG
Cora, WY 82925
(800)822-8466 or (307)367-4868
e-mail: info@boxr.com
Web: www.boxr.com
Season: June - September

Guest capacity: 25
Airport: Jackson Hole, WY

Ranch Based Horseback Vacations for Adults / Singles and Families.
If a working ranch vacation is your life long dream: and cowboys, good horses and gettin' up at dawn strikes your fancy, then we have the perfect get-away for you! Team up with your own personal four legged work partner for the week and join us movin' cattle, wranglin' the cavvy, riding for hours in the 840,000 acre Bridger National Forest and so much more! All-inclusive.

WYOMING
Powder River
Experience
P.O. Box 208
Clearmont, WY 82835
(888)736-2402   (307)758-4381 phone/fax

e-mail: prexp@mcn.net   Web: www.buffalowyoming.com/prexp/
Season: Year-round   Guest capacity: 12   Airport: Sheridan, WY, pickup available

Enjoy Authentic Western Cowboy Hospitality At Its Best.
Powder River Experience offers recreation on a 25,000 acre working ranch. Horse activities range from working with cattle during branding, calving, weaning to cattle drives. Other activities include overnight camping, fishing and watching wildlife. Come for sun or snow activities all year long. Our horses or yours. We will customize to fit your desires. Reservations suggested, call for availability.

WYOMING
Terry Bison
Ranch Resort
51 I-25 Service Road East
Cheyenne, WY 82007
(800)319-4171   (307)634-4171

Season: Year-round
Guest capacity: 23
Airport: Cheyenne, WY

**We are offering the only
Buffalo drive in the world!
Over 3,000 head and 25,000 acres!**
Hey tenderfoot - this is an authentic Buffalo

Drive so don't expect a mint on your pillow! This 1800's ranch was home to many historical figures including Teddy Roosevelt. Step back in time and experience the wide open prairie on horseback, pushing America's last hero to new pasture. Our accommodations include the updated original bunkhouse and 3 luxurious cabins, full service restaurant & bar, live entertainment, authentic Chuckwagon dinners, and trophy trout fishing. We house the first and only winery in Wyoming. So come experience the cowboy life!

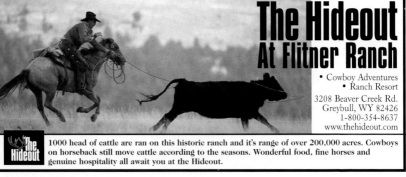

The Hideout
At Flitner Ranch
• Cowboy Adventures
• Ranch Resort
3208 Beaver Creek Rd.
Greybull, WY 82426
1-800-354-8637
www.thehideout.com

1000 head of cattle are ran on this historic ranch and it's range of over 200,000 acres. Cowboys on horseback still move cattle according to the seasons. Wonderful food, fine horses and genuine hospitality all await you at the Hideout.

WORLDWIDE RIDING VACATIONS

See the many sights of the world from horseback. Check with these companies to find the best in overseas travel.

CHINA / MONGOLIA / TIBET
Boojum Expeditions ⊤ ⛢

14543 Kelly Canyon Road
Bozeman, MT 59715
(406) 587-0125 (406) 585-3474-fax
E-mail: boojum@mcn.net
Web: www.boojumx.com

Season: June to October
Airport: Beijing, China
Guest Capacity: 14

Fourteen Years of Extraordinary Travel on Horseback with China's Nomadic Cultures.
Boojum Expeditions pioneered horseback treks in China, Tibet and Mongolia in 1984 and continues to lead rides in the remote corners of Central Asia, with the world's oldest nomadic horse-based cultures. Each itinerary includes 7-10 days of riding and lodging it tents and yurts, camping in a spectacular setting with nomadic herdsmen for our guides. Sample authentic meals. We ride an average of 15-20 miles per day. Join us for the equestrian adventure of a lifetime!

IRELAND
The Connemara Trail ⛢

The Aille Cross Equestrian Center
County Galway, IRELAND
U.S. representative:
Laura Pray, Crazy Oaks Farm
Rt. 2, Box 331B
Charleston, WV 25314
(800) 757-1667

Season: Year-round
Airport: Shannon, Ireland

Riding English and Western We offer a Variety of Ways to Experience Ireland on Horseback.
Join us to enjoy trekking across the magical mountains and beaches of Connemara, learn more about cross-country jumping or spend a few days foxhunting with the Galway Blazers. We have vacations to suit all levels of riders and can help arrange activities for non-rider companions as well. Ireland is a great spot for golf and fishing.

IRELAND / EUROPE / ENGLAND / ITALY SCOTLAND / WALES / FRANCE / SPAIN / COSTA RICA

Cross Country International 🏇

P.O. Box 1170
Millbrook, NY 12545
1-800-828-TROT (8768)
Season, airports, guest capacity varies
with destination.

Training Holidays with Expert Instruction.
Train in cross-country jumping, show jumping,
dressage and carriage driving. In England, Scotland, Wales, Ireland, France and Spain.

Trail Riding Holidays. Supervised and unsu-
pervised trail rides in England, Scotland, Wales, Italy, France, Spain and Costa Rica. Bed & breakfast
and hotel accommodations available Inn to Inn or one location.

MEXICO

Saddling South 🤠 Baja Pack Trips

P.O. Box 827
Calistoga, CA 94515
1-800-398-6200
(707) 942-4550 phone/fax

e-mail: tourbaja@iname.com
web: www.tourbaja.com
Season: October-May   Guest Capacity: 3-8
Airport: Loreto, or Baja California Sur, Mexico.
Airport pickup available.

Grab Your Sombrero for an Incredible Journey, into the Heart of the Sierra Giganta.
Saddling South takes you along volcanic ridges, through cactus garden valleys and into the lush palm
springs in Baja's spectacular desert mountains. Owner Trudi Angell, with 20 years experience
exploring this magnificent peninsula, offers a chance to learn traditions and histories of the remote
ranching lifestyle unique to Baja, Mexico. Join us as our local guides share their wisdom and lore
along the original missionary trails of the Californias.

Mongolia and Tibet Horseback Adventures

Ride with the world's oldest horse-based cultures through unfenced,
unsurpassed scenery. Multi-day pack trips with horses, camels and
yaks. Since 1985.

Boojum Expeditions
14543 Kelly Canyon Road
Bozeman, MT 59715 USA
Tel. 406-587-0125
Fax 406-585-3474

Reference Section

For More Information

Professional associations of qualified businesses can help in your search for the perfect horseback vacation. Contact these organizations for information about their membership.

Dude & Guest Ranches and Lodging Associations

The Dude Ranchers' Association
P.O. Box 471
LaPorte, CO 80535-0471
(970) 223-8440

Arizona Dude Ranch Association
P.O. Box 603
Cortaro, AZ 85652
Fax: (520) 744-7628

**Colorado Dude &
Guest Ranch Association**
P.O. Box 300
Tabernash, CO 80478-0300
(970) 887-3128

Montana Big Sky Ranch Association
1627 West Main St, Suite 434
Bozeman, MT 59715

**Wyoming Homestay (WHOA)
& Outdoor Adventures**
P.O. Box 40048
Casper, WY 82604
(307) 237-3526

British Columbia Guest Ranch Assoc.
P.O. Box 4501
Williams Lake, BC, Canada V2G 2V8
(800) 663-6000

Outfitters & Guides Associations

**Colorado Outfitters &
Guides Association**
2400 RBC RD 12
Meeker, CO 81641
970-878-4043

**Idaho Outfitters &
Guides Association**
P.O. Box 95
Boise, ID 83701
(208) 342-1919

**Montana Outfitters
& Guides Association**
Box 1248
Helena, MT 59624
(406) 449-3578

**Back Country
Horsemen of America**
P.O. Box 597
Columbia Falls, MT 59912

**Back Country
Horsemen of Montana**
P.O. Box 5431
Helena, MT 59604

**Oregon Outdoors
Association**
P.O. Box 10841
Eugene, OR 97440
(800) 747-9552

**Washington Outfitters
& Guides Association**
704 - 228th NE, Suite 331
Redmond, WA 98053
(425) 392-6107

**Wyoming Outfitters
Association**
P.O. Box 2284
Cody, WY 82414
(307) 527-7453

State Horse Councils

State horse councils can often offer information to the traveller looking for horse facilities and trails. Join your state horse council to strengthen the need for trail systems, the more of us to be counted the more need is seen by government, the more trails we have to enjoy in the future. List current at publication, December 1998. Some area codes may have changed.

American Horse Council
1700 K Street N.W., Suite 300
Washington, D.C. 20006
(202) 296-4031

Alaska State Horsemen
P.O. Box 141886
Anchorage, AK 99514-1886

Arizona State Horseman's Assn.
P.O. Box 31758
Phoenix, AZ 85046-1758
(602) 867-6814

Arkansas Horse Council
921 E. 5th St
Texarkana, AR 75502-5419
(870) 774-8822

California State Horsemen's Assn.
325-B Pollasky Avenue
Clovis, CA 93612-1139
(209) 325-1055

Colorado Horsemen's Council
220 LivestockExchange Bldg.
Denver, CO 80216
(303) 292-4981

Connecticut Horse Council, Inc.
P.O. Box 905
Cheshire, CT 06410-0905
(860) 659-0848

Delaware Equine Council
P.O. Box 534
Camden, DE 19934
(302) 398-5196

**(Florida) Sunshine State
Horse Council, Inc.**
P.O. Box 4158
North Fort Meyers, FL 33918-4158
(914) 731-2999

Georgia Horse Council
P.O. Box 736
Dahlonega, GA 30533-0736
(706) 542-7023

Horsemen's Council of Illinois
6 N. Walnut
Villa Grove, IL 61956
(217) 832-8419

Idaho Horse Council
5000 Chinden Blvd., Suite F
Boise, ID 83714
(208) 323-8148

Indiana Horse Council, Inc.
225 S. East Street, Suite 738
Indianapolis, IN 46202
(317) 692-7115

Iowa Horse Industry Council
1817 E. 30th
Des Moines, IA 50317
(515) 266-4734

Kansas Horse Council
1895 East 56 Road
Lecompton, KS 66050-4776
(913) 887-6422

Kentucky Horse Council
4089 Iron Works Pike
Lexington, KY 40511
(502) 695-8940

Maine Equine Industry Assn.
4 Gabriel Dr, RR 4, Box 1254
Augusta, ME 04330-9441
(207) 622-4111

Maryland Horse Council, Inc.
P.O. Box 4891
Timonium MD 21093-4891
(301) 252-2100

Massachusetts Horsemen's Council
97 Walnut Street
E. Douglas, MA 01516
(508) 476-3895

Bay State Trail Riders Assn.
24 Glenn Street
Douglas, MA 015116-2410
(508) 476-3960

Michigan Horse Council
P.O. Box 22008
Lansing, MI 48909-2008
(517) 676-0122

Minnesota Horse Council
13055 Riverdale Dr. NW
Box 202
Coon Rapids, MN 55448

Mississippi Horse Council
1924 McCullough
Tupelo, MS 38801-9721
(601) 842-9346

Missouri Equine Council
P./O. Box 692
Columbia, MO 65205-0692
(800) 313-3327

Montana Horse Council, Inc.
672 Airport Rd
Stevensville, MT 59870
(406) 777-2579

Nebraska Horse Council
P.O. Box 81481
Lincoln, NE 68501
(402) 434-8550

New England Horsemen's Council
2032 E. Main Road
Portsmouth, RI 02871-1226
(401) 683-1764

New Hampshire Horse Council
273 Poor Farm Rd
ipswich, NH 03071
(603) 878-1694

New Jersey Horse Council, Inc.
25 Beth Drive
Moorestown, NJ 08057-3021
(609) 231-0771

New Mexico Horse Council, Inc.
P.O. Box 10206
Albuquerque, NM 87184-0206
(505) 344-8548

New York State Horse Council, Inc.
189 Strawtown Road
New City, NY 10956

North Carolina Horse Council
6921 Sunset Lake Road
Fuquay-Varina, NC 27526
(919) 552-3536

Ohio Horseman's Council
P.O. Box 316
Miamisburg, OH 45343-0316
(740) 653-0466

Oregon Horse Council
P.O. Box 234
Cheshire, OR 97419-0234
(541) 998-2803

Pennsylvania Equine Council
P.O. Box 570
Bealsburg, PA 16827-0570
(814) 364 -9826

South Carolina Horsemen's Council
P.O. Box 11280
Columbia, SC 29211
(803) 734-2210

South Dakota Horse Council
45971 244 Street
Colton, SD 57018-5010
(605) 446-3613

Tennessee Horse Council
P.O. Box 69
College Grove, TN 37046-0069
(615) 395-7650 or (615) 297-3200

Utah Horse Council
1170 West 1000 South
Logan, UT 84321
(801) 752-7701

Virginia Horseman's Council
P.O. Box 148
Danville, VA 24541
(804)791-5706

Washington State Horse Council
P.O. Box 40263
Bellvue, WA 98015-4263
(360) 769-8083

Wisconsin State Horse Council
1675 Observatory Drive
287 Animal Science Bldg.
Madison, WI 53706-1284
(608) 263-4303

Please note, that area codes have been changing faster than we can keep up with them!

United States Trail Systems

Here is a partial listing of places with horse trails across the U.S., open to riders with their own mounts. Contact them directly for information on their trailheads, maps, camping facilities and trail mileage.

State Tourism offices have limited information on horse trails and state parks, we are including them as a source but be advised that they know more about golf, swimming and biking than horseback riding. Although information was provided by the states, please note, that area codes have been changing faster than we can keep up with them!

We are looking for additional information on public horse trails, and horseman's camps. Please mail information to us at Riding Vacations, Inc. P.O. Box 502, Richfield, OH 44286. or callus at (330) 659-6007. We would like trailheads, miles of horse trail, camping information and an address and phone number for more information.

ALABAMA– Tourism 1-800-252-2262
National Forests in Alabama
Montgomery, AL – (205) 832-4470
Oak Mountain State Park
Pelham, AL – (205) 620-2520
Talladega National Forest
Heflin, AL – (205) 350-6639
William Bankhead National Forest
Double Springs, AL – (205) 489-5111

ALASKA – Tourism - (907) 465-2012
Chugach National Forest
Anchorage, AK – (907) 271-2500
Denali State Park
Wasilla, AK – (907) 733-2675
Tongass National Forest
Sitka, AK – (907) 747-6671

ARIZONA – Tourism 1-800-842-8257
Alamo Lake State Park
Wenden, AZ 85357 (520)669-2088–Camp
Apache-Sitgreaves National Forest,
Springerville, AZ – (520) 333-4301
Catalina State Park
Tucson, AZ – (520) 674-5500

Chiricahua National Monument,
Wilcox, AZ (520) 824-3560 – 15 miles trail
Coconino National Forest,
Flagstaff, AZ – (520) 556-7400
Coronado National Forest
(602) 428-4150
Dead Horse Ranch State Park,
Cottonwood, AZ (520) 634-5283
Kaibab National Forest
Williams, AZ – (520) 635-2681
Grand Canyon National Park
Grand Canyon, AZ (520) 638-7809
Lost Dutchman State Park,
Apache Junction, AZ (520) 982-4485
Navajo National Monument
Tonalea, AZ (520) 672-2366
Petrified Forest National Forest,
Petrified Forest, AZ (520)524-6228
Prescott National Forest,
Tucson, AZ (520) 445-1762
Tonto National Forest,
Phoenix, AZ (602) 225-5200

ARKANSAS – State Tourism 1-800-643-8383

Bear Creek Trail
Jessieville, AR (501) 767-5715
Buffalo National River,
Harrison, AR (501) 741-5443 – 75 miles
Bull Shoals State Park,
Bull Shoals, AR (501) 431-5521
Devil's Den State Park
(501) 761-3325 – 25 miles trail, camp
Hot Springs National Park,
Hot Springs, AR, – 75 miles
(501) 624-3383 ext. 622
Mill Creek Park, AR,
(501) 637-4174, camp
Moccasin Gap Trails, Hector, AR
(501) 284-3150 campground
Mt. Magazine, Paris, AR
(501) 963-3076 – 40 miles, primitive camp
Pea Ridge National Military Park,
Pea Ridge, (501) 451-8122 – 11 miles
Ouchita National Forest,
Hot Springs, AR (501) 321- 5202
Ozark National Forest,
Russellville, AR (501) 968-2354

CALIFORNIA – Tourism–1-800-862-2543

Angeles National Forest
Arcadia, CA – (818) 574-1613
Burney Falls State Park
Burney, CA – (916) 335-2777
Cleveland National Forest,
Rancho Bernardo, CA – (619) 673-6180
Eldorado National Forest
Placerville, CA – (916) 644-6048
Golden Gate National Recreation Area
San Francisco, CA – (415) 556-0561
Humbolt Redwoods State Park,
Weott, CA (707) 946-2409
Inyo National Forest,
Bishop, CA – (760) 873-5841
Joshua Tree National Park
Twentynine Palms, CA –
(760) 367-7511
Kings Canyon National Park
Kings Canyon, CA 93271 –
(209) 335-2856
Klamath National Forest,
Yreka, CA – (916) 842-6131

Lassen National Forest,
Susanville, CA – (916) 257-2151
Los Padres National Forest,
Goleta, CA – (805) 683-6711
Mendocino National Forest,
Willows, CA – (916) 934-3316
Modoc National Forest,
Alturas, CA (916) 233-5811
Plumas National Forest,
Quincy, CA – (916) 283-2050
Point Reyes Nat'l Seashore,
Pt. Reyes, CA – (415) 669-1250 – 50 mi.
Redwood National Park
Crecent City, CA – (707) 464-6101
San Bernadino National Forest,
San Bernadino, CA – (714) 383-5588
Santa Monica Mountains
National Recreation Area
Agoura, CA – (818) 597-1036, ext. 231
Sequoia National Forest,
Porterville, CA – (209) 784-1500
Sequoia National Park
Three Rivers, CA – (209) 565-3341
Shasta-Trinity National Forests,
Redding, CA – (916) 246-5222
Sierra National Forest,
Clovis, CA – (209) 487-5155
Six Rivers National Forest,
Eureka, CA – (707) 442-1721

Stanislaus National Forest,
Sonora, CA – (209) 532-3671
Tahoe National Forest,
Nevada City, CA – (916) 265-4531
Tioyabe National Forest,
Bridgeport, CA – (619) 932-7070
Whiskeytown - Shasta-Trinity
National Recreation Area
Whiskeytown, CA – (916) 246-1225

COLORADO – Tourism 1-800-433-2656
Arapaho and Roosevelt Nat. Forests
Fort Collins, CO – (970) 498-1100
Colorado State Forest Park,
Walden, CO – (970) 723-8366
Golden Gate Canyon State Park,
Golden, CO – (303) 592-1502
Grand Mesa, Uncompahgre
&Gunnison National Forests
Delta, CO – (970) 874-7691
Pike & San Isabel Nat. Forests
Pueblo, CO – (719) 852-5941
Rio Grande National Forest
Monte Vista, CO (719) 852-5941
Rocky Mountain National Park
Estes Park, CO – (970) 586-1399
Routt National Forest
Steamboat Sprgs, CO – (970) 879-1722
White River National Forest
Glenwood Sprgs, Co – (970) 945-2521

CONNECTICUT – Tourism 1-800-282-6863
Collins Huntington State Park,
Hartford, – (860) 566-2304 – 878 acres
Hopeville Pond State Park,
Jewett City, CT –
Natchaug State Forest,
Eastford, CT – (860) 379-2469
Pauchaug State Forest,
Voluntown, CT – (860) 376-4075

DELAWARE – Tourism 1-800-441-8846
Bellevue State Park,
Diver, DE – (302) 739-4702
Cape Henlopen State Park,
Dover, DE – (302) 739-4702
Delaware Seashore State Park,
Dewey Beach, – (302) 227-2233

FLORIDA – Tourism (904) 487-1462
Blackwater River State Forest,
Rt 1, Box 77, Milton, FL camp
Florida Caverns State Park,
Marianna, FL – (904) 482-9598, 7 miles
Fort Cooper State Park,
Inverness, FL – (904) 726-0315 – 7 miles
Highlands Hammock State Park,
Sebring, FL – (941) 386-6094 – 11 miles
Jonathan Dickinson State Park
Hove Sound, FL–(561)546-2771
Little Manatee River State Rec. Area,
Wimauma, FL – (813) 671-5005– 6 miles
Myakka River State Park,
Sarasota, FL – (813) 361-6511 – 12 miles
Ocala National Forest, Eustis, FL,
(904) 357-3721–100 miles, primitive camp
O'Leno State Park
High Springs, FL – (904) 454-1853
Paynes Prairie State Preserve,
Micanopy, FL – (352) 466-3397 – 14 mil
Rock Springs Run State Reserve,
Sorrento, FL, – (352) 383-3311– 14 miles
Tallahassee-St Marks
Historic Railroad State Trail
Tallahassee, FL – (904) 922-6007
Tenoroc Fish Management Area
Lakeland, FL – (941) 499-2422

Tosohatchee State Reserve,
Christmas, FL –(407) 568-5893 – 23 miles
Wekiwa Sprgs State Park
Apopka, FL – (407) 884-2006 – 9 miles
Withlacoochee State Forest,
Brooksville, FL – campground

GEORGIA – State Tourism 1-800-847-4842
A.H. Stephens State Park
Crawfordsville, GA, – (706) 456-2602
Chickamauga and Chattanooga
National Military Park
Fort Oglethorpe, GA – (706) 866-9241
Hard Labor Creek State Park
Rutledge, GA – (706) 557-3001
Kennesaw Mountain
National Battlefield Park
Kennesaw, GA – (770) 427-4686
National Forests in Georgia,
Gainesville, GA – (404) 536-0541
Watson Mill Bridge State Park
Comer, GA – (706) 783-5349

HAWAII – Tourism (808) 586-2550
Haleakala National Park
Makawao, HI – (808) 572-4400

IDAHO – State Tourism 1-800-635-7820
Boise National Forest,
Boise, ID –(208) 373-4100 – 1,000 miles
Bruneau Dunes State Park
Mountain Home, ID –(208)373-4007
Cariboo National Forest,
Pocatello, ID – (208) 236-7500
Challis National Forest,
Challis, ID – (208) 879-2285
Clearwater National Forest
Orofino, ID –(208) 476-4541
Harriman State Park
Island Park, ID –(208) 558-7368 – 20 mi.
Hell's Gate State Park
Plummer, ID– (208) 686-1308 – 10 miles
Heyburn State Park
Plummer, ID–(208) 686-1308 – camp
Nez Perce National Forest
Grangeville, ID – (208) 983-1950

Payette National Forest,
McCall, ID – (208) 634-8151
Salmon National Forest,
Salmon, ID – (208) 756-2215
Sawtooth Nat. Rec. Area,
Ketchum, ID – (208) 726-7672
Targhee National Forest,
St. Anthony, ID – (208) 624-3151

ILLINOIS – Tourism - 1-800-223-0121
Argyle Lake State Park
Colchester, IL (309) 776-3422
Big River State Forest
Keithsburg, IL – (309) 374-2496
Camp Cadis-Shawnee National Forest
Harrisburg, IL – (618) 253-7114
Catlin Park of LaSalle County
Ottawa, IL – (815) 434-0518
Chain O'Lakes State Park
Spring Grove, IL – (847) 587-5512
Shawnee National Forest,
Harrisburg, IL – (618) 253-7114

INDIANA – State Tourism 1-800-289-6646
Brown County State Park
Nashville, IN – (812) 988-6406
49 mi, camp
Clark State Forest,
Henryville, IN – (812) 294-4306
Potato Creek State Park
North Liberty, IN – (219) 656-8186
Versailles State Park
Versailles, IN – (812) 689-6424
Wayne-Hoosier National Forests,
Bedford, IN– (812) 275-5987

IOWA – State Tourism – 1-800-345-4692
Iowa State Horse Trail Guide,
Iowa Dept. of Nat. Resources, (515) 281-5145

KANSAS – State Tourism –1-800-252-6727
Hillsdale State Park
Paola, KS – (913) 783-4507 – 30 miles
Milford State Park
Milford, KS – (913) 238-3014 – 8 miles
Perry State Park
Ozakie, KS – (913) 246-3449 – 30 miles

KENTUCKY – Tourism – 1-800-225-8747
Daniel Boone National Forest,
Winchester, KY – (606) 745-3100
Land Between the Lakes Nat. Rec Area,
Golden Pond, KY – (502) 924-2000
Mammoth Caves Nat. Park,
Mammoth Cave, KY – (502) 758-2328
Taylorsville Lake State Park
Taylorsville, KY– (502) 477-8766

LOUISIANA – Tourism - 1-800-334-8626
Kisatchie National Forest
Pineville, LA – (318) 473-7160

MAINE – Tourism - 1-800-533-9595
Acadia National Park
Bar Harbor, ME (207) 288-3338

MARYLAND – Tourism - 1-800-543-1036
Chesapeake & Ohio Canal
Sharpsburg, MD (301) 739-4200
Pocomoke River State Forest
Snow Hill, MD (410) 632-2566
Potomac-Garrett State Forest
Oakland, MD (301) 334-2038
Savage River State Forest
Grantsville, MD (301) 895-5759
Tuckahoe State Park
Queen Anne, MD (410) 820-1668

MASSACHUSETTS – Tourism - (617) 727-3201
Beartown State Forest
Monterey, MA (413) 528-0904
Erving State Forest
Erving, MA (508) 544-3939
Harold Parker State Forest
North Andover, MA (508) 686-3391
Horseneck Beach State Rec.
Westport, MA (508) 597-8802
Kenneth Dubuque State Forest
Charlemont. MA (413) 339-5504
Maudsley State Park
Newburyport, MA (508) 465-7223
Nickerson State Park
Brewster, MA (508) 896-3491
Savoy Mountain State Forest
North Adams, MA (413) 663-8469

Willard Brook State Forest
West Townsend, MA (508) 597-8802
Wompatuck State Park
Hingham, MA (617) 749-7160

MICHIGAN – Tourism - 1-800-5432-YES
Brighton State Recreation Area
Howell, MI (810) 229-6566
Hiawatha National Forest,
Escanaba, MI – (906) 786-4062
Highland Recreation Area
Milford, MI (810) 685-2433
Huron-Manistee National Forests,
Cadillac, MI – (616) 775-2421
Little Bay de Noc Grand Island Trail
Rapid River, MI (906) 474-6442
Lonia State Recreation Area
Lonia, MI (616) 527-3750
Mansitique Ranger District
Rapid River, MI (906) 474-6442
Ortonville State Recreation Area
Ortonville, MI (810) 627-3828
Ottawa National Forest,
Ironwood, MI – (906) 932-1330
Pontiac Lake Recreation Area
Waterford, MI (810) 666-795-9081
South Branch Shore to Shore Trail
Oscoda, MI (517) 739-0728
Yankee Springs Recreation Area
Middleville, MI (616) 795-9081
Waterloo Recreation Area
Chelsea, MI (313) 475-3170

MINNESOTA – Tourism - 1-800-657-3700
Arrow Head State Trail
Tower, MN (218) 753-6256
Camden State Park Horse Camp
Lynd, MN (507) 865-4530
Chippewa National Forest,
Cass Lake, MN – (218) 335-2226
Forrestville State Park
Preston, MN (507) 352-5111
Glacial Lakes State Park
Starbuck, MN (612) 239-2860
Heartland State Trail
Nevis, MN (218) 652-4054

Lac Qui State Park
Montevidoe, MN (612) 752-4736
Lake Louise State Park
LeRoy, MN (507) 324-5249
Maplewood State Park
Pelican Rapids, MN (218)863-8383 -20 mi
Mille Lacs Kathio State Park
Onamia, MN (320) 532-3523 - 25 miles
Minnesota Valley Rec. Area
Jordan, MN (612) 492-6400 - 35 miles
North Shore State Trail
Two Harbors, MN (218) 834-5238
Pillsbury State Forest
Brainerd, MN (218) 828-2565
Sibley State Park
New London, MN (612) 354-2055
St. Croix State Park
Hinckley, MN(320) 384-6591 - 75 miles
Superior National Forest,
Duluth, MN (218) 720-5324
Taconite State Trail
Tower, MN (218) 753-6256
Wild River State Park
Center City, MN (612) 583-2125

MISSISSIPPI – Tourism - 1-800-647-2290
Bigfoot Horse Trails
McHenry, MS (601) 428-0594
Longleaf Horse Trails
Laurel, MS (601) 428-0594
Mississippi National Forests,
Jackson, MS (601) 965-4391

MISSOURI – Tourism - 1-800-877-1234
Cuivre River State Park
Troy, MO (573) 528-7247
Dr. Babler State Park
Chesterfield, MO (573) 458-3813
Knob Noster State Park
Knob Noster, MO (816) 563-2463
Mark Twain National Forest,
Potosi, MO (314) 438-5427
Rolla, MO (314) 364-4621
Sam A. Barker State Park
Patterson, MO (5730 856-4411

MONTANA – Tourism - 1-800-541-1447
Beaverhead National Forest
  Dillon, MT (406) 683-3900
Bitteroot National Forest
  Hamilton, MT (406) 363-3131
Bob Marshall Wilderness
  Bigfork, MT (406) 837-5991
  Choteau, MT (406) 466-5341
Custer National Forest
  Billings, MT (406) 657-6361
Deerlodge National Forest
  Butte, MT (406) 496-3400
Flathead National Forest
  Kalispell, MT (406) 755-5401
Gallatin National Forest
  Bozeman, MT (406) 587-6701
Helena National Forest
  Helena, TM (406) 449-5201
Kootenai National Forest
  Libby, MT (406) 791-7700
Lolo National Forest
  Missoula, MT (406) 329-3750
Scapegoat Wilderness
  Lincoln, MT (406) 362-4265

NEBRASKA – Tourism - 1-800-228-4307
Fort Robinson State Park
  Crawford, NE (308) 665-2660
Indian Cave State Park
  Shubert, NE (402) 883-2575
Nebraska National Forest
  Chadron, NE (308) 432-0300
Niobra State Park
  Niobra, NE (402) 856-3373
Ponca State Park
  Ponca, NE (402) 755-2284
Rock Creek Station State Park
  Fairburty, NE (402) 857-729-5777

NEVADA – Tourism - 1-800-237-0774
Humbolt National Forest,
  Elko, NV (702) 738-5171
Toiyabe National Forest,
  Austin, NV (702) 964-2671
  Carson City, NV (702) 482-6286
  Sparks, NV (702) 355-5301

NEW HAMPSHIRE – Tourism - (603) 271-2666
Bear Brook State Park
  Concord, NH (603) 485-9874
Pawtuckaway State Park
  Concord, NH (603) 895-3031
Pisgah State Park
  Concord, NH (603) 239-8153
White Mountain National Forest
  Laconia, NH (603) 528-8721

NEW JERSEY – Tourism - 1-800-JERSEY-7
Allaire State Park
  Farmingdale, NJ (908) 938-2371
Beleplain State Forest
  Woodbine, NJ (609) 861-2404
Delaware & Raritan Canal State Park
  Somerset, NJ (908) 873-3050
Wharton State Forest
  Mannonton, NJ (609) 561-0024

NEW MEXICO – Tourism 1-800-545-2040
Carson National Forest
  Taos, NM – (505) 758-6200
Cibolo National Forest
  Albuquerque, NM – (505) 761-4650
Gila National Forest,
  Silver City, NM (505) 388-8201
Horse Mountain Wilderness
  Socorro, NM (505) 835-0412
Lincoln National Forest
  Alamogordo, NM (505) 437-6030
Santa Fe National Forest,
  Santa Fe, NM – (505) 988-6940

NEW YORK – 1-800-1-800-225-5697
Brookfield Trail,
  Sherburn, NY (607) 674-4067 – 130 miles
Catskill Forest Preserve
  Albany, NY (518) 457-7433
Finger Lakes National Forest
  Ithaca, NY (607) 594-2750
Otter Creek Horse Trail,
  Lowville, NY – (315) 376-3521 – 43 miles
Phillips Creek Trail,
  Belmont, NY – (716) 268-5392 – 15 miles

NORTH CAROLINA -Tourism - 1-800-VISIT - NC
Bladen Lakes State Park
(910) 588-4964
Blue Ridge Parkway
Laurel Springs, NC (910) 372-8568
Cane Creek & Union County Parks
Waxhaw, NC (704) 843-3919
Cedar Rock County Park
Graham, NC (910) 570-6760
Croatan National Forest
New Bern, NC (919) 638-5628
Great Smokey Mountains National Park
Cherokee, NC (615) 436-1200
Hanging Rock State Park
Danbury, NC (910) 593-8480
Latta Planatation Park
Huntersville, NC (704) 875-1391
Leatherwood Mountains
Ferguson, NC (910) 973-4142
Love Valley Trails
Love Valley, NC (704) 592-2024
Morrow Mountain State Park
Albemarle, NC (704) 882-4402
Moses Cone Memorial Park
Blowing Rock, NC (704) 295-3782
Nantahala National Forest
Robbinsville, NC (704) 479-6431
North Carolina National Forests,
Asheville, NC (704) 257-4200
Old College Farm Trail
Shelby, NC (704) 484-1731
Pilot Mountain State Park
Pinnacle, NC (910) 325-2355
Pisgah National Forest
Hot Springs, NC (704) 622-3202
Raven Rock State Park
Lillington, NC (910) 893-4888
Sertoma Tails
Danbury, NC (910) 983-4757
South Mountains State Park
Connelly Springs, NC (704) 433-4772
Stone Mountain State Park
Roaring Gap, NC (910) 957-8185
Tanglewood Park
Clemmons, NC (910) 766-9540

Uwharrie National Forest
Troy, NC (910) 576-6391
Weymouth Woods-Sandhills Preserve
Southern Pines, NC (910) 692-2167
William B. Umstead State Park
Raleigh, NC (919) 787-3033

NORTH DAKOTA – Tourism- 1-800-437-2077
Fort Abraham Lincoln State Park
Mandan, ND (701) 663-4758
Ft. Ransom State Park
Ft. Ransom, ND (701) 973-4331
Little Missouri State Park
(701) 764-5219
Maah Daah Hey Trail,
Medora, ND (701)225-5151, 120 miles
Sheyenne National Grasslands
Bismark, ND (701) 683-4342
Sulley Creek Recreational Area
Bismark, ND (701) 683-4342
Theodore Roosevelt National Park, South
Medora, ND (701)623-4466 – 36 miles
Theodore Roosevelt National Park, North
Watford City, ND (701) 842-2333
Turtle Mountain State Forest
Arvilla, ND (701) 594-4445

OHIO – 1-800-BUCKEYE
Alum Creek State Park
Delaware, OH (614) 548-4631 – 50 miles
Beaver Creek State Park, E. Liverpool, OH
(330) 385-3091 – 23 miles, camp
Blue Rock State Park
Blue Rock, OH (740) 674-4794 – 26 miles
Ceasar Creek State Park, Waynesville, OH
(513) 897-3055 – 25 miles, camp
Cleveland Metroparks,
Cleveland, OH (216) 351-6300 – 83 miles
Cuyahoga Valley Nat. Rec Area,
Brecksville, OH 1-800-433-1986 - 20 miles
East Fork State Park
Bethel, OH (513) 734-4325 – 57 mi, camp
Great Seal State Park
Waynesville, OH (740) 773-2726 - 17 miles
Hocking State Forest
Rockbridge, OH (740) 385-4402 - 40 miles

Lake Hope State Park
Zaleski, OH (740) 596-5253 - 33 miles
Malabar Farm State Park
Lucus, OH (419) 892-2784 12 miles, camp
Mohican State Park
Loudonville, OH - 30 miles
Oak Openings State Park
Toledo OH (419) 535-3050 - 15.5 mi
Paint Creek State Park
Bainbridge, OH (513) 365-1401 - 25 miles
Shawnee State Forest
Portsmouth, OH - 75 miles
Salt Fork State Park
Cambridge, OH (740) 439-3521 -25 miles
Tar Hollow State Forest
Laurelville, OH (740) 887-4818
West Branch State Park
Ravenna, OH (330) 296-3239-20 miles

OKLAHOMA – Tourism – 1-800-652-6552
Ouachita National Forest
Ouachita Nat. For., (918) 653-2991 – 70 mi.
Robber's Cave State Park
WIlburton, OK (918) 465-2565
Talimenta State Park
Talihina, OK (918) 567-2052

OREGON – Tourism – 1-800-547-7842
Bullard's Beach State Park
Coos Bay, OR (503) 347-2209
Deschutes National Forest,
Bend, OR (503) 388-2715
Fremont National Forest,
Lakeview, OR (503) 947-2151
Herman Creek Trail
Gresham, OR (503) 666-0700
Malheur National Forest
John Day, OR (503) 575-1731
Milo Melver State Park
Estacada, OR (502) 222-2223
Mount Hood National Forest
Gresham, OR (503) 666-0700
Nehalem Bay State Park
Nehalem, OR (503) 368-5154
Ochoco National Forest,
Prineville, OR (503) 447-6247

Rogue River National Forest,
Medford, OR (503) 776-3600
Silver Falls State Park
Salem, OR (503) 873-8681
Siskiyou National Forest
Grants Pass, OR (503) 479-5301
Siuslaw National Forest,
Corvallis, OR (503) 750-7000
Table Rock Wilderness
Salem, OR (503) 375-5646
Umatilla National Forest,
Pendleton, OR (503) 276-3811
Umpqua National Forest
Roseburg, OR (503) 672-6601
Wallowa-Whitman National Forest
Baker City, OR (503) 523-6391
Willamette National Forest
Eugene, OR (503) 465-6521
Winema National Forest
Klamath Falls, OR (503) 883-6714

PENNSYLVANIA –Tourism– 1-800-VISIT-PA
Allegheny National Forest,
Warren PA (814) 723-5150
Blue Knob State Park
Imler, PA (814) 276-3576
Moraine State Park
Portersville, PA (412) 368-8811
Pennsylvania State Parks
Harrisburg, PA (800) 63-PARKS
Wyoming State Forest
Bloomsburg, PA (717) 387-4255

RHODE ISLAND – Tourism (800) 556-2484
Arcadia Management Area
Richmond, RI (401) 277-1157

SOUTH CAROLINA –Tourism (803) 734-0122
Baker Creek State Park
McCormick, SC (803) 443-2457
Croft State Park
Spartanburg;, SC (864) 585-1283
Francis Marion-Sumter National Forest,
Columbia, SC (803) 765-5222
Greenville County Recreation Area
Greenville, SC (864) 288-6470

Kings Mountain State Park
Blacksburg, SC (803) 222-3209
Lee State Park
Bishopville, SC (803) 428-3833
Palmetto Trails
Columbia, SC (803) 771-0870
SOUTH DAKOTA – Tourism: 1-800-843-1930
Black Hills National Forest
Custer, SD (605) 673-2251
Custer State Park
Cister, SD (605) 255-4515
George S. Mickelson Trail
Deadwood to Edgemont, (605) 773-3391
Newton Hills State Park
Canton, SD (605) 987-2263
Oakwood Lakes State Park
Bruce, SD (605) 627-5441
Shade Hill Recreation Area
Shade Hill, SD (605) 374-5114
Sica Hollow State Park
Lake City, SD (605) 448-5701
Union County State Park
Beresford, SD (605) 253-2370

TENNESSEE – Tourism – (615) 741-2158
Big South Fork National Recreation Area
Oneida, TN (615) 879-4890
Cherokee National Forest,
Cleveland, TN (615) 476-9700
Great Smokey Mountains National Park
Gatlinburg, TN (615) 436-5615
Lone Mountain State Forest
Wartburg, TN (423) 346-6655
Natchez Trace State Park
Wildersville, TN (901) 968-3742

TEXAS – Tourism – 1-800-8888-TEX
Angelina National Forest
Lufkin, TX (409) 639-8620
Big Bend National Park,
Big Bend, TX (915) 477-2251
Caprock Canyons State Park
Quitaque, TX (806)445-1492
Davy Crockett Nat. Forest,
Crockett, TX (409) 544-2046 – 50 miles

Guadalupe Mountains Nat. Park,
Salt Flat, TX (915) 828-3251 – 80 miles
Hill Country State Area,
Bandera, TX (210) 796-4413, 34 miles
Lake Arrow Head State Park
Wichita Falls, TX (817) 528-2211
Lake Somerville Park,
Somerville, TX, (409) 535-7763 – 26 miles
Palo Duro Canyon State Park
Canyon, TX (806) 488-2556 – 22 miles
Sabine National Forest
Cleveland, TX (409) 275-2632
Sam Houston Nat. Forest,
Cleveland, TX (713) 592-6461

UTAH – Tourism – (801) 538-1030
Ashley National Forest,
Vernal, UT (435) 789-1181
Bryce Zion Grand Canyon Parks
Tropic, UT (435) 679-8665
Canyon Rims Recreation Area
Monticello, UT (435) 587-2141
Dixie National Forest,
Cedar City, UT (435) 586-2421
Fishlake National Forest,
Beaver, UT (435) 438-2436
Loa, UT (435) 836-2811
Richfield, UT (435) 896-4491
Uinta National Forest,
Provo, TU (801) 377-5780
Wasatch-Cache National Forests,
Salt Lake City, UT (801)5030

VERMONT – Tourism – (802) 828-3236
Green Mtn. & Finger Lakes Nat. Forest
Rutland, VT (802) 773-0300
Gronton State Forest
Marshfield, VT (802) 584-3820

VIRGINIA – Tourism – 1-800-VISIT-VA
Carter Taylor Mulit-Use Trail
Buckingham County (804) 983-2175
Cumberland Multi-Use Trail
Cumberland County
Fort Pickett
Blackstone, VA (804) 292-2613

Fort Valley
Fort Valley, VA (888) 754-5771
Fountainhead Park
Fairfax Station, VA (703) 250-9124
George Washington National Forest
Deerfield Ranger Dist. - (540) 885-8028
Dry River Ranger Dist. - (540) 828-2591
James River Ranger Dist - (540) 962-2214
Lee Ranger Dist - (540) 984-4101
Warm Springs District - (540) 839-2521
James River State Park
Blacksburg Ranger Dist. - (540) 552-4641
Clinch Ranger District - (540) 328-2931
Glenwood Ranger Dist. - (540) 291-2188
Wythe Ranger Distrct - (540) 228-5551
Jefferson National Forest
Blacksburg, VA (703) 552-4641
Roanoke, VA (703) 982-6270
Manassas National Battlefield Park
Manassas, VA (703) 754-8694
Mt Rogers National Recreation Area
Marion, VA (540) 783-5196
New River Trail State Park
Austinville, VA (703) 699-6778
Mt. Rogers National Recreation Area
Marion, VA (703) 783-5196
New River State Park
Austinville, VA (540) 699-6778
Pettigrew Trail
Buckingham County (804) 292-2613
Pohatan Wildlife Management Area
Pohatan, VA (804) 598-4286
Prince Edward-Gallion Multi-Use Trail
Prince Edward County (804) 983-2175
Robertr Mufort Trail
(804) 738-6143
Stauton River State Park
Halifax County (804) 572-4623
Shenandoah National Park
Luray, VA (703) 999-2266
Virginia Creeper Trail
Abingdon, VA (800-) 435-3440
W&OD Railroad Regional Park
Ashburn, VA (703) 689-1437

WASHINGTON – Tourism – 1-800-544-1800
Beacon Rock
Vancouver, WA (509) 427-8265-13 mi.
Bluff Mountain Trail
Yacolt, WA (360) 427-5645
Colville National Forest
Colville, WA (509) 684-3711
Iron Horse Trail
North Bend, WA (360)426-9226 - 113 mi
Gifford Pinchot National Forest
Vancouver, WA (206) 696-7500
Huffman Peak & Siouxon Trails
Amboy, WA (360) 247-5473
Mt Baker-Snoqualmie National Foerest
Mountlake Terrace, WA (206) 775-9702
Okanogan National Forest
Okanogan, WA (509) 826-3275
Olympic National Forest
Olympic, WA (206) 956-2300
Steamboat Lake State Park
Grand Coule Dam, WA (509) 633-1304
Sun Lake State Park
Soap Lake, WA (509) 246-1821
Wenatchee National Forest
Wenatchee, WA 98801 (509) 662-4335

WEST VIRGINIA – Tourism – (304)348-2286
Babcock State Park
Clifftop, WV (304-425-9481
Monongahela National Forest,
Elkins, WV (304) 636-1800
North Bend Rail Trail
Cairo, WV (304) 643-2931
Valley Falls State Park
Fairmont, WV (304) 367-2719

WISCONSIN – Tourism – (608) 266-2161
Ahnapee State Trail
Kewaunee City, WI (414) 746-2890
Bailey Lake Equine Trail
Three Lakes, WI (715) 479-2827
Black River State Forest
Black River Falls, WI (715) 284-1426
Brule River State Forest
Douglas County, WI (715) 372-4866

Buffalo River Trail
Mondovi, WI (608) 534-6409
Chequamegon National Forest,
Park Falls, WI (715) 362-3415
Eu Claire County Forest
(715) 839-4738
Governor Dodge State Park
Grantsburg, WI (715) 463-2898
Governor Knowles State Park
Grantsburg, WI (715) 463-2898
High Cliff State Park
Appleton, WI (414) 989-1106
Kettle Moraine State Forest
Kewaskum, WI (414) 626-2116
La Riviere Park
Prairie du Chein, WI (608) 326-6445
Nicolet National Forest,
Rhinelander, WI (715) 362-3415

Mt Valhalla Recreation Area
Washburn, WI (715) 373-2667
Otter Springs Trail
Cranmdon, WI (715) 478-3475
Tri-County Recreation Corridor
Tri-County WI (715) 373-6125
Wildcat Mountain State Park
Ontario, WI (608) 337-4775
Wild Goose State Trail
Dodge City, WI (414) 386-3705

WYOMING – Tourism – 1-800-661-8888
Bighorn National Forest
Sheridan, WY (307) 672-0751
Bridger-Teton National Forest
Jackson, WY (307) 733-2752
Medicine Bow National Forest
Laramie, WY (307) 745-8971
Shoshone National Forest
Cody, WY (307) 527-6241

Vacation Consultation

The Best Way to Vacation
is on the Back of a Good Horse...

I firmly believe that there is no better way to vacation. Why be "bored sitting around on a beach" when you could be riding. There is nothing like a gallop down a beach. As you ride along you really get to see your surroundings, feel the wind on your face, listen to the streams splashing over rocks, the sound of the birds, and smell the pine forest around you. Go any other way and you have obstructions to these enjoyments. Hike and you must look down at the ground to place your next step. Ride a bike and you must be youthful in the best of condition. Take a motorcycle and smell the fumes and drown out your surroundings with noise.

There are many types of horseback vacations. No two are exactly alike. Not every place will be to your liking, some may be too rustic, others too formal. Sometimes it is hard to decide from afar. Each year I get out to visit many of the places in this book. I would be happy to share my first-hand knowledge of horseback vacations with you to help you find a great vacation.

What I need to know is what you want. How many riders are in your party or will you be vacationing alone? Where would you like to go? What price range are you looking for? Do you want to fly or drive to your destination?

Please fill out this form send it or fax it to me and I will be happy to help you. To request our free brochure of Riding Vacations Adventures, (places that we have most recently tested), check off the box for that purpose. We will be happy to help you make reservations to any of the places listed. This is a free service for you. By coming through Riding Vacations you will get the best possible price on your vacation. Phone 330-659-6007 or fax 330-659-6706.

Custom Vacations from Riding Vacations, Inc.

We will be happy to custom match you to a vacation site beyond those in our Riding Vacations Advntures brochure. In doing so we accrue a certain amount of expense for our time, and mailing expenses and need to charge a **REFUNDABLE $25 fee** for doing so. Let us help you with your reservations, your fee will be refunded at that time.

Contact Information: ☐ Please send me a free copy of the Riding Vacations Adventure Brochure

Name _____ Date _____

Address _____

City/State/Zip _____

Phone (_____) _____ home (_____) _____ work

Tell us what you are looking for in a riding vacation. _____

_____

_____

_____

RIDING VACATION PROFILE

I wish to ride _____Western _____English _____I will ride either

Experience level: _____beginner _____intermediate _____advanced

Type of vacation I most want to enjoy: _____

Part of country: _____

Dates I wish to travel _____ to _____

How many in your party: _____ Ages: _____

Do you have non-rider companions joining you? _____ Yes _____ No

How do you like to travel to your destination? _____ your car _____ airline _____ rental car

What else do you want to do while you are there? _____

Custom Vacation Planning ($25). Please charge it to my credit card

VISA / Master Card #_____ _____ _____ _____ exp. date _____

Signature _____ date _____

Making Reservations Through
Lynne Johnson & Riding Vacations, Inc.

We are happy to help you find the proper destination for your riding vacation. Call us. We will be happy to discuss your wishes and help match you with just the right site.

Call us for our free brochure of vacations we have personally tested for quality. Reservations on these trips are made at no extra charge to you.

We can answer any questions you may have, tell you of availability of space and put a hold on that space until you get your deposit in. Use the form below to sign up. Just fill it out and send it in to Riding Vacations with the proper deposit. (Call us to find out space availability and deposit amount)

Customized packages

Please call the Riding Vacations office at 330-659-6007. Tell us where you wish to vacation, dates that you wish to be there and number of people in your party. There will be a $25 charge for custom trip preparation. This will include assorted brochures, reservations and airline/car rental ticketing.

Thank you for making your reservations through Riding Vacations.

Vacation Reservations

Please include this form with your reservations, Copies acceptable.
Please reserve space for me on the following ride. I wish to vacation at:

_____ in _____ Vacation Date_____to_____
State

Name_____ Date_____ Deposit included_____

Address_____

City/State/Zip_____

Phone (_____) _____ home ( ) _____work

| Rider(s) | birthdate | height | weight | Riding Experience | | |
				extensive	moderate	beginner
1.						
2.						
3.						
4.						

In making this reservation, I certify that there is some risk involved in a horseback vacation in general as well as wilderness or backcountry travel over remote trails. I realize that helmets are a way of increasing my safety, and should I not decide to wear one while riding it is my decision. I understand that Lynne Johnson and Riding Vacations are only involved in the booking of my riding trip and are not responsible for the horses assigned, trails ridden, my safety or personal happiness. My safety is completely in the hands of the ride operator and will not hold Lynne Johnson, or Riding Vacations, Inc. responsible for any accidents which may occur.

Signatures of all riders_____ _____

_____ _____Date_____

Send completed form with your deposit check to:
Riding Vacations, Inc. • P.O. Box 502 • Richfield, OH 44286 • (330) 659-6007

Vacation Report

The Horse Lovers Vacation Guide wants to know how your vacation went.
Please copy this form to give us a report of your trip.

Your name and address_____

_____

Place you vacationed – (Name/address)_____

_____

Date of your stay _____ Was this your first horseback trip?___Yes ___ No

Did the Horse Lovers Vacation Guide help you to find your destination? ———————

Tell us about this years vacation. (Horses, riding, accommodations, meals) _____

_____

_____

_____

_____

_____

_____

_____

What other horseback vacations have you taken? (name and address of place) _____

_____

Would you recommend the destination? __ Yes __ No Why? _____

_____

How can we make future HLVG editions more usable to you? _____

_____

Do you have a copy of the Riding Vacations Adventure Schedule (free)?
We would be happy to send you a copy.

For another copy of the Horse Lovers Vacation Guide?
Send $9.95 +$3 (US funds)postage to address below.

phone (330) 659-6007
Riding Vacations, Inc. • P.O. Box 502 • Richfield, OH 44286 USA • (330) 659-6706 fax

"The Best Way to Vacation is On The Back of a Good Horse!"

– Lynne Johnson

Pack trip in the Canadian Rockies – *Holiday on Horseback*